RESEARCHWATCHING
Lifting the lid on market research

About the author

Our specially commissioned study shows that Giles Lury has considerable experience in brands, marketing and research, having worked in advertising, brand consultancy, packaging and corporate identity.

It also identified that he is currently a Partner at HPI Research Group, where he heads up the international Research Division. We know that somewhere along the way he managed to win two IPA Advertising Effectiveness Awards and a gold award at the AMSO Research Effectiveness Awards.

We discovered that he is also a regular contributor to many trade and national publications and has appeared on BBC radio and TV as a brand 'guru'. His two previous books are *Brandwatching* and *Adwatching* (both published by Blackhall Publishing).

Giles is happily married with five children, which we note means that he can run his own children's mini-groups whenever necessary.

Giles welcomes comments or questions about his work and can be contacted at: giles.lury@hpiresearch.com

RESEARCHWATCHING

lifting the lid on market research

Giles Lury

BP

BLACKHALL
Publishing

This book was typeset by
Ashfield Press Publishing Services for

BLACKHALL PUBLISHING
33 Carysfort Avenue
Blackrock
Co. Dublin
Ireland

e-mail: info@blackhallpublishing.com
www.blackhallpublishing.com

© Giles Lury, 2004

ISBN: 1 842180 84 3

A catalogue record for this book
is available from the British Library.

Printed in Ireland by
ColourBooks Ltd

To the one in ten cats

who don't prefer the taste of Whiskas

Contents

Acknowledgements

Whilst only my name appears on the front of this book, it would never have been completed without a great deal of help from many friends and colleagues.

Some of those who deserve a special mention include Robert Sjøborg, director of the Orkla Brand School. He asked me to write *A Guide to Market Research* for him and his students. It was a great spur to go on and write *Researchwatching*. With his kind permission, I have also directly used some of that guide in writing this book.

Thanks also to friends and colleagues at HPI including Paul Laver, Luca Dogliotti, Jo Rodger, Terry Prue, Juliet Strachan and Marie Parkes, but especially David Iddiols for reading the manuscript not once, but twice, and then providing valuable suggestions and some great case histories.

Gavin Galloway, a one-time colleague at The Value Engineers, provided me with a great deal of advice, experience, expertise and the occasional beer for which he has my gratitude. Phil Spires of Vegas Research and Brand Development helped with advice, encouragement and the occasional enlightening anecdote.

I should also like to thank Stephen Wells of Wells and Co. I have probably seen Stephen run more focus groups than I would care to remember but his skilful handling of them has taught me an awful lot about qualitative research as well as providing me and my clients with numerous insights.

Alistair Cummings, who I worked with at Springpoint, helped me write the Orkla *Guide to Market Research*. Fenella McCarthy helped more than perhaps she realises, as I discussed numerous aspects of market research with her over the years we worked together at Springpoint.

Dawn Childs kindly provided me with some of the cartoons for which she has my thanks and envy – I wish I could draw.

I would like to thank David Barr of the MRS and Peter Mouncey formerly of the MRS.

I would also like to thank all the companies and agencies that have kindly let me reproduce pictures and logos.

And as ever I would like to thank my wife, Karen, who both sense-checks and proofreads all that I write. Without her help this would probably make a lot less sense!

Introduction

Nowadays there are lies, damn lies and market research. In today's consumer-driven society it's no longer any old statistics, but what the latest market research says that really matters.

It may be clichéd, but knowledge is power and for an increasing number of companies, market research is a key source for that knowledge. It has become a vital tool for management. Unfortunately many would also say it is an overvalued, overused, often misinterpreted and rarely fully understood tool.

From being cross-examined in the street about your choice of toilet paper to being the basis for TV game shows such as *Family Fortunes*, it is also obvious that market research is now everywhere. Companies research what their names should be, whether or not we like and understand their advertising and how often we use their existing products and services. They use research to develop ideas for new products and services and much more besides.

Market research has become prevalent in just about every industry there is. There are few manufacturing or service companies, retailers, media houses, advertising agencies, government departments, public bodies or academic institutions that do not regularly use market research in some shape or form.

Indeed some social observers like Andrew Neill, former editor of *The Sunday Times*, believe we are now living in a country run, not by a government, but by focus groups! And when Tony Blair, the British Prime Minister, and the leader of the opposition resort to using quotes from the aforementioned focus groups to goad each other at *Prime Minister's Question Time*, you have to wonder whether there is some truth in the assertion. Can you imagine an election without polls and pollsters? There would be so little to talk about they might even have to discuss the issues and proposed policies!

Research even plays a role in highly creative industries

such as film-making. The original proposed ending for *Fatal Attraction* was slated in pre-release research and the 'finale' was re-scripted, re-shot and re-edited.

In a world where many marketing decisions can be worth millions of pounds, market research at least provides an opportunity to 'look before you leap'. It can cost millions to develop and launch a new product, embark on a new marketing strategy or advertising campaign and some earlier research can help guide their development and execution.

Before buying a house, doesn't everyone undertake a survey?

From humble origins the market research industry in the UK alone is now estimated to be worth over £600 million a year, employing many thousands of people and conducting over 12 million interviews every year. Founded in 1946 by 23 individuals, The Market Research Society now has around 8,000 members.

Researchwatching sets out to analyse this fast-growing industry. It aims to look at those who make a living out of looking at us and reporting on that to others. What is market research? Why is it done? How is it done? Does it really help people make better decisions?

Each of the chapters is relatively self-contained, answering the question in its title, and so can be read in any order you choose. If you have a good grasp of the alternative methodologies or if you want a more discursive break from the meatier methodological chapters then it might be advisable to skip ahead and read some of the later chapters earlier.

Whichever order you read it in, I hope you firstly enjoy the book and secondly get something from it.

What is market research?

It has often been said that the difference between a sales-led and marketing-led approach to business is that in a sales-led approach you sell what you make, whilst in a marketing-led approach you produce what you know you can sell. An underlying assumption in the marketing-led approach therefore is that there is some process by which you learn about what will sell. That process is market research. It is more fully defined by Wendy Gordon and Roy Langmaid in their book *Qualitative Research* as:

> *A process whereby information about the behaviour and/or attitudes of consumers or end users of a product or service is collected by means of some form of interrogatory procedure.*

It was defined by Philip Kotler in *Principles of Marketing* as:

> *The systematic design, collection, analysis and reporting of data relevant to a specific marketing situation facing the company.*

David Iddiols, Senior Partner at HPI, describes it more straightforwardly as:

> *Finding out what real people actually think and do, rather than assuming you know what they think and do.*

And P. Kleinman defined it, somewhat circularly and perhaps a little cynically, as:

> *What market research agencies do.*

However, like many other definitions of market research, these focus on the 'process', the activities of market research, rather than on its objectives. At the most basic level market research aims to help management make better decisions by providing information relating to markets and marketing. Hence, the MRS (Market Research Society) defines market research as:

> *The means used by those who provide goods and services to keep themselves in touch with the needs and wants of those who buy and use those goods and services.*

The idea of 'keeping in touch with' or of 'being close to' your consumer is an often-quoted argument in favour of market research. Charles Handy, in his widely read book *In Search of Excellence*, cites keeping close to customers as one of the crucial factors that helped make the companies he surveyed so successful.

Whilst staying close to the consumer is a key role for market research it is by no means the only role. Gavin Galloway of The Value Engineers describes and segments the roles of research as:

> *UMEP – understanding, measuring, explaining and predicting.*

His model is based on linking the roles of research back to the needs of marketing managers. He identifies four key tasks where market research plays a vital role:

> **Understanding** *customers and their needs*
> **Understanding** *and* **measuring** *the competitive context*
> **Predicting** *the forces of change*
> **Predicting, measuring** *and* **explaining** *the outcomes of alternative marketing and brand actions (strategy and/or tactics).*

Understanding is specifically to do with:

◆ understanding the underlying motivations/attitudes that drive consumer behaviour
◆ understanding specific consumer responses to our market and the brands within it.

Measuring is, as the name suggests, all to do with the measurement or quantification.

Explanation is to do with the notion of explaining in the scientific sense, for example: How much did x contribute to y?

Prediction can be sub-divided into two areas, specific/short-term and broad/long-term.

◆ The short-term or specific prediction is about generating estimates of what will happen as the result of a specific action or actions. It can therefore be seen as the opposite of an explanation. Explanations in a market research context try to explain why something has happened and what the specific effect of each of the key variables (for example pricing, advertising, competitive activity, the launch of a new product) has been. The short-term prediction looks at what might happen in the future as certain key variables are changed.

◆ The long-term/broad prediction is similar in that it relates to the future but takes a more macro/big-picture perspective. It encompasses trend analysis and prediction and the more recently named 'futurology'.

Galloway therefore believes that:

> *Research is not a corporate objective or strategy and it should not be a replacement for management judgement. Rather it can be seen as a 'map' of the commercial terrain and some of the potential routes across. It should help the manager to understand, measure, optimise, choose and sometimes predict.*

What he is saying is that while understanding, measuring, evaluating and predicting are the roles for market research, they are not the end benefit. As mentioned earlier the real benefit of market research is to help management make better decisions. In *A Handbook of Market Research Techniques* Birn, Hague and Vangelder state:

> *Market research is a means of providing management with market and marketing information. Its main purpose is to:*
>
> ◆ *Reduce uncertainty when marketing strategy is being planned*

◆ *And to monitor performance after the strategy has been put into operation.*

As many have noted, however, the quality of any market research depends largely on the definition of the problem it is being used to address. It is possible to research just about anything but whether or not that information is useful is the crucial issue when it comes to applying the results. As Harding and Walton note in *Bluff your Way in Marketing*:

> *The usefulness of any research is not measured by its inherent quality but by the ability of those on the receiving end to do something about it.*

Indeed there is an old saying that market research can be used as a drunk uses a lamppost – either as illumination or for support. Most companies claim to know the difference and to use it to guide but a surprising number use it as a crutch to try to help them make difficult decisions.

Before leaving the subject of the definition of 'market research', it is worth noting three further issues surrounding the issue. Firstly, while in common practice the phrases marketing research and market research are interchangeable, there is, or rather was, a formal distinction between them. Market research was originally formally defined as finding out information relating to a specific market for a particular product or service. This was therefore a very specific and rather narrow definition of research. Marketing research, however, has a much broader definition, which Peter Chisnall gives in *Marketing Research*:

> *It covers product development, identifying the market, and suitable methods of selling, distribution, promotion, and sales/service facilities. In fact, every aspect of business activity from 'idea stage' to eventual consumer satisfaction [is covered]. [Marketing research] is by no means restricted to profit-motivated business activities. It has very useful applications in, for example, the development of charities, public sector leisure, and culture services, etc.*

Secondly, at various times people have looked at all that is covered by market research (or rather marketing research) and questioned whether 'market research' covers all that the discipline does. They take the argument further than differentiating between market and marketing asking whether either term is broad enough. Indeed, Sir Harold Wilson, when he was president of the MRS in 1979, suggested that market research might be more appropriately renamed 'attitude research' because as he noted 'politics is not a market'. Whilst this is undoubtedly true and continues to be pointed out by some observers, no one has yet come up with a new term that has been generally accepted.

Finally, given there has been some debate over the terms 'market', 'marketing' or some other term such as 'attitude', it is perhaps not surprising that other observers, for example Robert Buzzell in *Is Marketing a Science?*, have also expressed concern that the term 'research' is applied to this industry.

Buzzell's view is that the activities of market/marketing/attitude research are a long way from 'pure academic research' such as that conducted in a laboratory under controlled conditions. This is undoubtedly true and while market research does use some scientific methodologies, few would argue that marketing is a science and that market research, which happens in the 'real' world outside of the laboratory, is pure research.

Indeed, as will be discussed in later chapters, whilst the development of research owes much to many different disciplines, one that has had surprisingly little influence is that of economic theory. The main reason for this is that a lot of economic theory depends on the notion of an economic or rational being. Unfortunately in the real world, we, funny creatures that we are, do not always act rationally!

However, this lack of purity does not seem to have impeded market research's usefulness and has not stopped the rapid growth of the industry. As Harding and Walton in *Bluff your Way in Marketing* note:

> *Market research is the petrol of marketing ... it's expensive, damaging to the environment and will only take you so far. This has not prevented it from becoming one of the boom industries.*

2

How does market research impact on our lives?

Which would you choose?

Nowadays even the size of the melons you buy in your local supermarket is 'decided' by market research. As Libby Brooks reported in *The Guardian* on 3 May 1999:

Melons feel the squeeze at Tesco

The supermarket psychologists who brought us theories of trolley daze and aisle alignment, who calculate the relative spend increase induced by the stall of freshly baked bread, have surpassed themselves; they have entered the realm of the psycho-sexual.

As a consequence, Tesco, Britain's biggest supermarket chain, has asked its suppliers to grow smaller melons after focus groups of shoppers revealed that shoppers subconsciously selected fruit according to the trend in breast size.

After investigating a marked drop in melon sales, a retail psychologist's report for Tesco suggested the modern preference for smaller breasts, as modelled by the likes of superwaif Kate Moss, is informing customers' decisions to reject melons.

The company instructed growers in Spain to produce Galia melons of no more than 0.55kg, rather than the 1kg melons that were proving slow to sell.

A Tesco spokesman yesterday said the findings surprised him but insisted that the sales spoke for themselves.

'Since we introduced the smaller melons two months ago we have sold more than a million.'

The possibility of a subconscious relationship was first raised when a member of an all-female focus group, set up when Tesco buyers sought to find out why customers consistently picked the smallest fruit from store displays.

Despite the fact that you may never have been accosted in the street and asked to 'spare just a couple of minutes', market research impacts on all of our lives, every day of every week of every year. That is because while market research may include being cross-examined in the street about your choice of toilet paper or newspaper, it has also a host of other applications up to and including TV game shows such as *Family Fortunes*. Market research is simply everywhere.

Market research is used by companies to help them decide what their names, and the names of their brands, should be. Unilever tested the effect of changing from Jif to Cif; Mars tested the shift from Opal Fruits to Starburst. Even the ultimately ill-fated moves to Consignia (by the Post Office) and Monday (by PWC consulting) were researched.

Almost all of the ads we see on television and many of the press and poster ads will have been researched to see whether or not we like and understand them. That's not including the reams of research that is conducted to help the agencies understand the brand and their consumers better so that they can get to the brief for the development of the original creative brief.

Much of the packaging we see in supermarkets and shops and even the layout of those shops are researched. Research can be used to help evaluate what products should be placed where on the shelves to help a store, a brand or a category maximise its sales. Eye level just to the right of centre of an aisle is the best place to site a particular product. In one study I saw, this led to an increase of 17 per cent for the tested product.

There are numerous tracking studies to help companies assess how often we use their existing products and services and what our attitudes are to them. The media companies conduct exhaustive ongoing audience research into how many people watch, listen, see and 'visit' them and their programmes. It is their lifeblood, as it is on the basis of these figures that media planning and buying agencies will decide whether to use them. It also helps determine how much they are willing to pay to advertise in that specific media. If you know a particular show is regularly watched by five million of your target audience versus another show that is only watched by two million, then an advertising spot in the first is much more valuable. If the ratings (percentage of the population) are not high enough to help generate the desired revenue then it can sound the death knell for that programme or series.

Research even plays a role in development of the creative work for media. As mentioned earlier, it is even used on the biggest films. When researched, the director's proposed ending for *Fatal Attraction* did not 'play well', as they say in Hollywood. The test audiences felt there wasn't enough of a 'climactic finale', which were probably polite words for 'not enough blood'.

The studio insisted it was re-scripted, re-shot and re-edited with much more blood. The film went on to be a box office smash grossing over $80 million, much to the disgust of the director, Adrian Lynne, who later issued his director's cut of the film. Best-selling author Stephen King is known to use market research in his development process.

Market research or at least market research techniques are used widely by political parties, particularly in helping them develop their communication strategies. Many social observers now believe that this research has a much greater influence in shaping not just how the parties communicate but in deciding their policies. Indeed, some social observers like Andrew Neill, the editor of the Scotsman, believe we are now living in a country run, not by a government, but by focus groups!

New Labour and Tony Blair, the British Prime Minister, have been closely linked with the approach and the launch of their 'Big Conversation' programme in 2004 has further contributed to this perception. However, it is perhaps unfair to pinpoint them, as research has long been associated with politics – it is hard to imagine an election without polls and pollsters!

Indeed, research has become a vital tool in just about every industry. From life insurance to condoms, from frozen peas to tropical holidays, from the government to lobby groups like Greenpeace, there are few sectors that do not regularly use market research in some shape or form.

It has been reported that even the Royal Family has recently turned to market research as part of its drive to rebuild its image.

3
What are the main differences between qualitative and quantitative research?

Just suppose you want to investigate the men's toiletries market, what sort of questions would you like answered?

◆ How often do men shower?
◆ How often do they bathe?
◆ When do they bathe or shower – in the morning or evening or both?
◆ What products do they use?
◆ Do they use shampoos as well as conditioners?
◆ What brands do they use? How long does the average shower last?
◆ Do they use bar or liquid soaps?
◆ How do these figures compare with women's behaviour and men's behaviour in other countries?

Having established what they do and how often they do it
(and having been either horribly shocked or delightfully surprised), you might go on to ask questions about how they feel
about bathing in general. How do they view having a bath as
opposed to taking a shower? (Why do you *have* a bath yet *take*
a shower?) Why do they feel more positive to one brand than
another?

A short lesson in Latin

All of these and more are the standard sorts of questions that
are addressed by market research but reflect the two classic
disciplines. To understand this division all one needs is a short
lesson in Latin.

The two disciplines are quantitative and qualitative
research. *Quantitative research* derives its name from 'quanto',
Latin for 'by how much'. The name *qualitative research* origi-
nates from the Latin 'qualis', meaning 'of what kind, sort or
nature'. Thus, quantitative research can be seen to be primari-
ly concerned with the measurement of things, often called
'hard data', whilst qualitative research is centrally concerned
with trying to understand why things were, are or might be
and is known as 'soft data'.

At its core, quantitative research is concerned with seeking
the views and/or measuring the habits of large samples of
defined populations, whilst qualitative research uses smaller
samples but digs deeper, so can perhaps be expressed dia-
grammatically as follows:

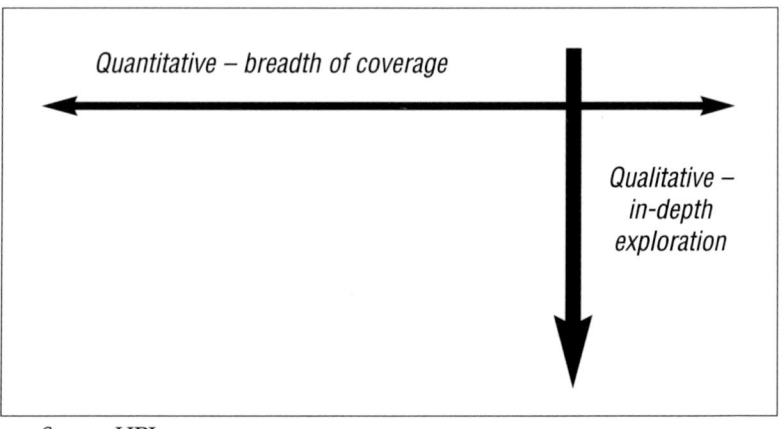

Source: HPI

In broad terms, qualitative research is used to *understand* and guide long-term predictions. Quantitative research is used to *measure* and then modelling of the data is used to either *explain* or *predict* (as in the case of stimulated market modelling). Trends measurement on a quantitative basis is also used in long-term prediction.

The main advantages of these two different disciplines can be summarised as follows:

Quantitative	Qualitative
Precise statistical and numerical measurement	Open-ended, flexible
Uses large, statistically representative samples	Provides greater depth of understanding
Can provide information that can be reliably analysed on sub-sample basis	Can get below rationalised or superficial responses
Provides consistent basis for analysis – surveys can be repeated at regular intervals	Can be used to tap consumers' creativity

Quantitative research

The MRS defines quantitative research as:

> *Conclusive evidence on relatively large samples for measuring the incidence of views and/or actions. Quantitative research can be descriptive or causal depending on the design.*

Quantitative research is fundamentally about answering 'How much?' and 'How many?' (*measure and explain*). It can then be used in *predicting* what might happen in the future (i.e. if x changes by a certain amount it can be extrapolated that y will change by z amount).

The primary reasons for choosing a quantitative methodology are:

◆ to provide a statistically robust guide to decision making
◆ when detailed analysis is required of sub-group of a given
  sample
◆ when data modelling is required.

Cynics might add:

◆ when you want to cover yourself against situations where
  things go wrong
◆ in companies that are 'numbers' driven.

The general characteristics of quantitative research are that it
is based on precise statistical and numerical measurement. As
in most cases it would be uneconomical or infeasible to interview the whole 'population' (for example 'all the users of a
particular brand' or 'everyone aged eighteen or over') then
the analysis is nearly always based on large statistically representative samples. Regular surveys are a major example of
quantitative research so another desired characteristic is that
it provides a consistent/replicable basis for analysis.
    Key applications for quantitative research include:

◆ To help measure key market and consumer characteristics.
  Most companies need to know the basic facts of their marketplace – how big it is, whether or not it is growing, how
  many people use it, what the demographics of those people
  are – to help them plan more effectively.

◆ To help measure the brand and market status and trends.
  What are sales, distribution, sales dynamics, brand awareness, usage and attitudes, and brand image of their and
  their competition's brands? This information is important
  in planning marketing and advertising.

◆ To help measure the effects of different brand actions and
  their effectiveness, such as promotions, pack changes, new
  product launches and advertising, so aiding future planning and budget allocation.

◆ To assess and predict the possible likely outcome of alternative options for future brand actions, so aiding decision
  making.

The main methodologies used will be explored in Chapter 6.

Qualitative research

Rudyard Kipling wrote about his 'six honest serving men', a group that teaches all of us what we need to know about market research:

> *I kept six honest serving men, who taught me all I knew. Their names were What and Why, and When and How, and Where and Who.*

But in defining qualitative research, Bandler and Grinder in *Frogs into Princes* seem to be obliquely referencing this:

> *Qualitative research answers such questions as 'What', 'Why' or 'How' but it cannot answer the question 'How many?'*

Harry Henry in *Motivational Research*, first published in 1958, eloquently puts the case for qualitative research with his now famous comparison of bikinis and statistics:

> *Parallel with the development of market research has grown up a gradual realisation that the basic facts of the market situation are not, by themselves, sufficient to **explain** that situation, or to indicate the most fruitful lines for production, marketing, and advertising activity. It is essential for these basic facts [to] be known, but they do not provide the whole answer.*

> *Indeed in the fields of marketing and advertising, statistics are like bikinis – they reveal a great deal that is both interesting and instructive, but they usually conceal what is vital.*

As discussed earlier qualitative research is focused on understanding motive and reason and so has different characteristics to the more mathematical approaches used in quantitative research. Gordon and Langmaid identify the general characteristics of qualitative research in so far as it

◆ *involves small samples of consumers, which are not necessarily representative of larger populations*

◆ *employs a wide variety of techniques to collect data, not simply a structured question-and-answer format*
◆ *relies on interpretation of findings, which is an integral part of data collection and indeed begins well before the fieldwork commences at the briefing*
◆ *allows access to the ways in which the consumers express themselves.*

This 'less rigorous non-scientific' approach with its emphasis on asking people what they feel and believe and on interpretation meant that, at least initially, qualitative research was met with some resistance. There is no hard data and it put the 'power' in the hands of consumer judgement rather than traditional knowledge or scientific judgement.

Despite these reservations the importance of the information provided means that qualitative research has grown and grown. The following are some of the most widely used applications:

◆ Basic exploratory studies
◆ New product development
◆ Creative development
◆ Diagnostic research.

Basic exploratory studies are undertaken to provide the fundamental information and hopefully some useful insights on how markets/brands/products are perceived. This sort of research aims to provide a better understanding of purchase and usage decisions: What is the decision-making 'process' people go through? How and why do people choose one brand over another?

New product development: research is used to help identify opportunities for improving existing products and provide guidance on how to develop concepts and early ideas for new products and services.

Creative development: consumer reactions are used to help develop and evaluate advertising, packaging and other communication ideas.

Diagnostic research: used when companies want specific input in understanding specific market and/or brand issues. As we have seen this includes a whole variety of issues, including why Tesco shoppers consistently chose smaller melons (see Chapter 2).

4

What are the main techniques of qualitative research?

The Golden Arches of the McDonald's M are one of the most instantly recognisable brand icons in the world. Children almost too young to speak can spot them and will point them out to their parents, imploring them to take them for a Happy Meal.

In his book *The Total Package*, Thomas Hine recounts the story of Louis Cheskin, a researcher who was working with McDonald's at a time when they were considering abandoning the arches as an architectural feature. While agreeing that it might be sensible to move away from arched windows:

> [Cheskin] advised that the memory of the arches be kept in the form of the M in 'McDonald's'. His case was based, he said, on research that 'the arches had Freudian applications to the sub-conscious mind of the consumer and were great assets in marketing McDonald's food'. In other words, Cheskin said, the arches are 'mother McDonald's breasts, a useful association if you're replacing home-made food'.

The story highlights the origins and 'backbone' of much qualitative research, even if it is a rather extreme example.

Much of qualitative research theory and many of its techniques have their basis in psychology. The key reason for this is that the central issue in qualitative research is the need to be reasonably certain that the researchers are getting an adequate and fair understanding of what the people's motivations and responses really are.

While there is no incentive for people to lie in a qualitative research situation, there are a number of reasons why their responses might not be as fully detailed or 'true' as those doing the research might like.

◆ There is a tendency for people to operate purely on a rational level. In a famous product test quoted in Harry Henry's *Motivational Research* people were given two packs of biscuits. They were told one was made with butter and the other without. The majority preferred the biscuits made with butter and gave reasons such as 'they were richer', 'they were creamier' and 'they were tastier'. The minority who preferred those made without butter said they found these biscuits 'more digestible' and 'less greasy'. These are all good reasons except of course they were given two identical packs of biscuits, demonstrating not only that people tend to give 'good' rational reasons but also that people say what they feel and believe not necessarily what is true.

◆ Group dynamics can influence individual responses. It is often the case that when the majority of a group say that they like something there is great pressure on the others to agree. There may be an unwillingness to divulge information or opinion beyond a certain point. Respondents may be unable or may not wish to express attitudes or feelings adequately. In certain cases, people may not be fully aware of their own motivations or responses. People may over- or under-claim on their behaviour to fit in with the rest of the group or to 'show-off'. I once did research into drinking stout in Ireland and when one bloke replied that his average weekly consumption was about 100 pints, I wasn't sure, particularly given his size, whether this was an under- or an over-estimate!

Wendy Gordon, a renowned researcher, summarised these factors in her book *Good Thinking: A Guide to Qualitative Research*:

> *The fundamentals of human psychology applied to marketing research: people will not share feelings and thoughts with a researcher if these are in any way embarrassing to self-esteem; that people are always trying to 'look good' (rational, intelligent, helpful); that some attitudes and emotions are difficult to put into words; that 'rationalisations', 'ambivalence', 'justifications', 'projections' are part of everyday human life.*

So to help avoid these possible issues, qualitative research borrowed and adapted techniques from clinical psychology that help overcome inhibition and facilitate free expression. These techniques, known as projective and enabling techniques (examples of which are given in Chapter 8), are defined by Gordon in *Good Thinking* as consisting of:

> *A situation or stimulus that encourages a person to project part of him or herself on to an external object or to bring it into the interview itself. In the context of qualitative market research, projective techniques are designed to enable the individual or group to express these feelings through light hearted and safe exercises, which reveal insight both to the individuals themselves as well as to the researcher.*

The aim of these techniques is to get beyond the stereotypical answers – the conventional or predictable responses – and any 'games' or defence systems to people's genuine thoughts and feelings.

Levels of consciousness

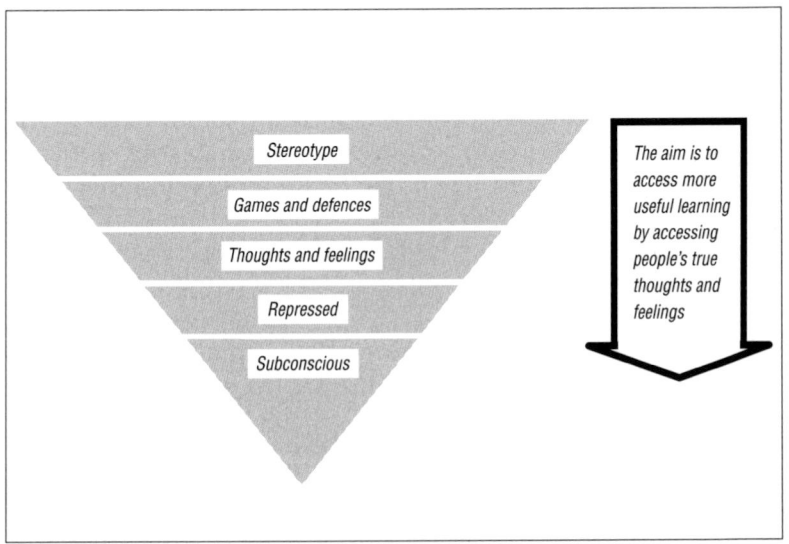

It is when qualitative research tries to push down into the lower levels of repressed and subconscious that it tends to be most open to question and/or ridicule. As Harry Henry said in *Motivational Research*:

> *When motivation research is used to establish, firmly and unequivocally, that a housewife is more likely to buy a product if it is packaged in a blue wrapper than a red one, it is doing a useful and worthwhile job; when it goes further, to discover that she prefers blue to red because she was frightened by a bull in early childhood, it is simply wasting time and resources.*

Qualitative research also relies heavily on the skills and experience of the moderator to help interpret and analyse the findings. For example, reading transcripts does not fully capture the tone of voice or body language of the respondents that in many cases can be more important than what was actually said.

Group discussions and *depth interviews* are currently the most commonly used qualitative research methods but many others exist and new ones are constantly being developed and evolved. Group discussions (also known as focus groups) are groups of seven to nine people in the UK. (In the US the standard group size is ten to twelve people.) People are brought together to exchange their personal experiences, attitudes and beliefs and to respond to selected stimulus materials about a particular market/brand/topic. Group discussions are a useful tool when investigating what participants – different types of people – think about a certain subject or issue and they are particularly suitable for discovering *why they think the way they do.*

One of the major strengths of group discussions is that they facilitate interaction. People can spark off one another, which can be particularly useful when conducting development research, as people will often build on what has been said before. It is important to realise that while groups can be useful for discussing many subjects, they are not suited to *all* subjects. Subjects of a personal or sensitive nature (i.e. personal hygiene) may be best explored outside of a group situation. Group discussions can be and often are viewed simultaneously from a viewing room by clients and agencies either via one-way mirrors or a video link.

There is an ever-growing number of variations on the standard discussion, the more accepted and widely used variations include:

Mini-groups, as the name suggests, are merely a smaller

version of a standard group discussion with four to six respondents. They are used either to allow for greater interaction or when there is a large amount of, or particularly complex, stimulus material. They are often used for business research.

Extended groups, or as they are sometimes called *extended creativity groups,* are run with six to eight respondents for longer periods and so allow greater depth of discussion and the use of more time-consuming and creative exercises such as image ripping (whereby respondents create their own image montages with pictures torn from magazines).

The extra time means that it is possible to 'educate' consumers so they can act more like creative consultants. This approach is often used in the early stages of new product development. It is also true to say that increasingly, as everyone has become more marketing literate, they are able if not extremely keen to 'play' at being marketers themselves.

Reconvened groups are groups recruited for two sessions separated by a week. The first week normally covers the key topics and initial views and/or expectations. In the second week the group can be asked to do a number of exercises and then to come back and discuss these and their analysis of them.

They are often used for concept testing or new product testing because they allow for groups to be recalled and views can be taken pre- and post-trial, as it is possible to explore spontaneous reactions to an idea/concept and then place sample products with the respondents and revisit the item to assess reactions once they have actually experienced it. Did it meet expectations? How did they actually use it?

Alternatively a group might be asked to stop doing something for a week – such as drinking tea and/or coffee – and then explore their reactions to this and what they did instead.

Conflict groups are another variation on standard groups whereby the sample is deliberately split into sub-groups with contrasting views, for example users of competing brands or users and non-users. Conflict groups are used to provoke a more lively and comparative debate of the key issues. Some people believe that the very relaxed, very friendly, non-confrontational atmosphere of most discussion groups does not encourage people to discuss their true feelings in enough

depth and that by deliberately setting up a situation to provoke debate and even argument, people's true feelings and
beliefs can be seen more clearly.

Beyond these widely used forms, agencies such as HPI have
pioneered the use of other variations on the theme such as
amoeba groups and *wind tunnel groups*. As the name implies,
amoeba groups split in two at an appropriate juncture, with
the resultant mini-groups run by two moderators. This
approach provides the opportunity to explore separately and
in more detail the views of, say, bitter drinkers versus lager
drinkers or 'likers' and 'dislikers' of a concept for a new advertising campaign. Wind tunnel sessions are often used at an
early stage of new product development work, wherein specially recruited articulate, creative consumers are gathered
together to provide initial responses and ideas around the con-
cept(s). I have recently heard mention of jacuzzi focus groups
but have not yet had the occasion to run one. (See Chapter 7
for more on group discussions and their popularity.)

Internet discussions are becoming increasingly popular. Using
either a notice board or chat room facility it is possible to get
reasonably large groups to discuss topics. However, these
discussions are not viewed by the moderator who therefore
cannot interpret/read non-verbal language and signals of any
group. Furthermore, unless participants are pre-selected and
only allowed secure access then there can be issues of authenticity about their replies.

Depth interviews are one-on-one interviews used where an in-
depth understanding of individual reactions to personal or
sensitive issues are required. They can also be highly relevant
where the sample group consists of individuals who are difficult to locate, spread across a large geographic area or are
high-powered individuals or specialists who may find it difficult to spare time for research (for example senior business
personnel, doctors and so on).
 Some of the main advantages and disadvantages of depth
interviews are summarised in the table overleaf:

Depth interviews	
Advantages	**Disadvantages**
◆Depth interviews as the name suggests allow the interviewer to explore the subject more deeply ◆Provide participants with the opportunity to give their personal opinions (and avoid the issues of group/peer pressure) ◆Provide an appropriate forum for the discussion of sensitive or personal issues ◆Minority and majority opinions can be voiced freely ◆Information can be gathered over a longer period of time from one respondent ◆The interviewer can break down a tendency for people to stop within socially accepted norms, behaviour and attitudes ◆The sample can be segmented and spread over more narrowly defined target groups than is practically possible with a focus-group approach ◆Can be well suited to a sample that is widely dispersed or severely time pressured	◆ Can be difficult to facilitate an exchange of creative thinking ◆ Are time consuming, both to conduct the interviews and to analyse the transcripts of the conversations ◆ Can be expensive for the reason given above

Group discussion and depth interviews can also be combined to good effect in many research programmes. For example, when researching the internal attitudes, feelings and culture of a specific company I have often combined a range of depth interviews amongst the senior management with a number of discussion groups among middle and junior employees.

Observational interviewing (based on ethnography) is literally living with people in real time; exploring their actual use of products and brands; sharing the minutiae of their behaviour and relationships with brands and products. It is currently a rapidly growing area of research, which although based on an even smaller sample is based on real not claimed behaviour. As one of the leading exponents, Siamack Salari of EverydayLives said in a recent *Sunday Times* article ('How would you feel if you learnt this man was 'studying' your rubbish?'):

> *It's not that focus groups don't want to help. It's that they don't (always) know how to. For instance, they don't know exactly what they do when they put their contact lenses in. I know, I've filmed them.*

Salari worked with Sainsbury's and two of his recommendations can be seen to have come from his observational interviewing:

> *He filmed a mother and son for two days before noticing [that] a drawer in the fridge contained all the family's non-allergic foods. He suggested that Sainsbury's, likewise, could dedicate an area of the store to its Free From range. At a children's party, he noted the son was miserable because there was no 'junk food'. Salari recommended Sainsbury's 'junk up' Free From, and make it more treat like.*

Like a number of other research techniques borrowed from 'academia' it is unlikely that what is currently being called 'ethnography' would meet the rigorous standards of its founder, the anthropologist Bronislaw Malinowski. He recommended that the ethnographer should spend at least a year in the field, use the local vernacular, live apart from his own 'kind' and above all make the psychological transference whereby 'they' becomes 'we'.

Accompanied sessions are a variation on observational interviewing whereby the interviewer 'accompanies' a respondent while they are 'performing' a single activity such as shopping, a journey, web surfing or a night out. They can provide a deeper understanding of decision making and usage. They are often used in retail situations to see how someone shops a particular sector or aisle compared with how they shop other sectors or aisles, or more broadly to compare and contrast how people shop in one supermarket and another.

Consumer workshops combine a number of aspects from more traditional research methods, for example focus groups with the techniques of brainstorming. They can also deliver against the increasing desire for direct client-consumer interaction (client participation in the actual research process) as well as delivering the need for speed.

The simplest way to envisage a consumer workshop is to imagine four or five miniature group discussions being run simultaneously but managed by a 'master of ceremonies' – an experienced moderator/facilitator who introduces the session, sets up each stage and chairs plenary sessions where the individual groups report back and comment on other groups' views.

They usually run for longer than traditional discussion groups as the increased number of people and the need to interact necessitates more time. Workshops often run for four or five hours whilst most discussion groups run for one-and-a-half to two hours. Having a number of different mini-groups means that different perspectives or levels of usership can be included in the one session, bringing with it some of the benefits of conflict groups.

The diagram below shows how a consumer workshop might be set up:

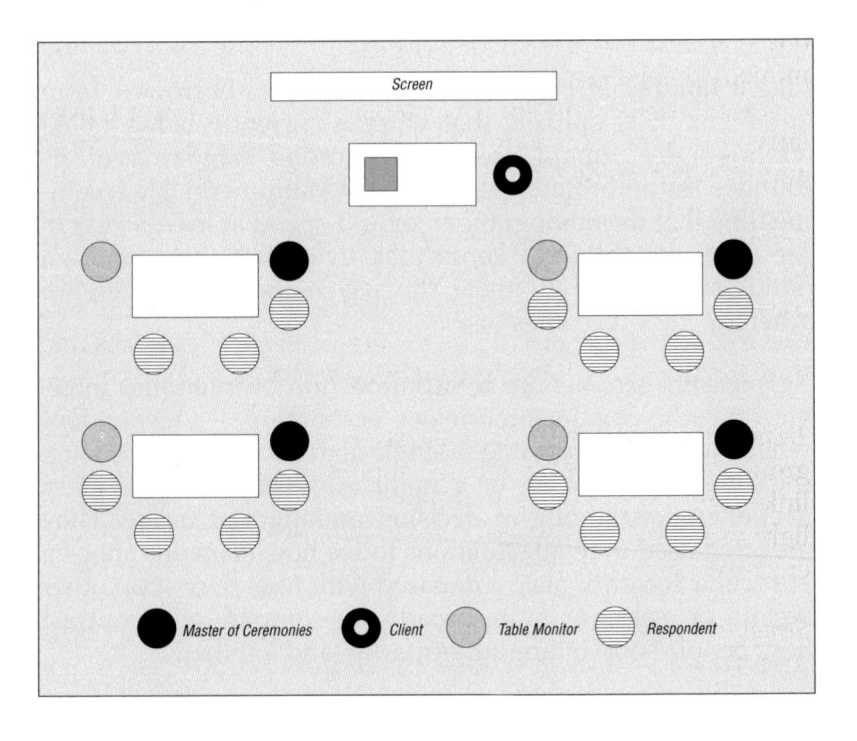

As the diagram shows, a client or agency member sits on each table amongst the respondents and is involved in all the discussions. This is obviously very different to discussion groups where these people are traditionally behind a one-way mirror, if present at all. Whilst this changes the dynamics of the research it can be very valuable to client and agency people who participate.

As David Walker, a partner at innovation consultancy, Synectics, notes in an article in *brand strategy* ('*Where have all the big ideas gone?*'), marketers often take more notice of consumers' opinions when they are in the same room as them rather than on the other side of a two-way mirror. Walker recalls one teenager bluntly telling a marketing VP that his brand wrapper looked like a piece of crap.

> *The executive was taken aback and then exclaimed 'God, you're right!' He asked his research manager why this had slipped through. It hadn't. It had been cited in every report over the last five years but had been ignored by the marketing department.*

The fact that there are a number of mini-groups being run simultaneously (and that the clients are involved) can speed up the process. A number of groups have been conducted in one day and with their involvement clients can give a more immediate feedback.

Two situations where consumer workshops are particularly appropriate are rapid immersion in a new marketplace and innovation/new product development projects.

Paired depths are a variation on depth interviews and are particularly appropriate if exploring brands targeted at couples, if the subject matter is 'dry' or if a single respondent might feel exposed if on their own. With young or difficult samples and vulnerable groups, friendship pairs may be a sensible option.

Triangular/triads are perhaps most often used as mini-conflict groups whereby each respondent holds a different view or is linked with competitive brands. For example, a heavy user, a light user and a lapsed user or where each belongs to a different bank/shop or a different supermarket.

Semiotic analysis aims to read the 'hidden' meaning of marketing messages. It is a more theoretical and academic approach to decoding the unconscious signals and signs a brand is sending out and so revealing that brand's (and its marketers') unconscious beliefs about its consumers and the marketplace. Advertising and other images, language, media content and packaging design are evaluated to understand the cultural framework within which purchasing patterns have developed and been influenced.

A semiotic analysis of much of traditional whiskey advertising conducted in the era when every campaign seemed to feature a glowing, cosy fireside suggested that the original 'firewater' had been 'emasculated' and put behind the fireguard. Whilst this had become a cultural norm it was not appealing to younger audiences at all, who were in fact much more drawn to powerful imagery. Not surprisingly, whiskey advertising has changed significantly since then. It uses specialist techniques to try to overcome the (culturally) conditioned or expected responses by providing a deeper understanding of people's real motivations.

Whilst semiotic analysis can sometimes lead to new and powerful insights, it is also more open to ridicule as it often relates beliefs and actions to more basic and often sexual motivations. For example, a semiotic analysis of the appeal of eating chocolate likened it to suckling mothers' milk.

Telephone interviews are sometimes used when researching samples of business and other busy people, where there are simpler objectives and where no stimulus materials are required. (It is a little difficult to present a concept board over the phone.) Whilst it is possible to have the type of open-ended, free-flowing discussion that characterises qualitative research, the researcher does not have the benefit of watching and interpreting the participant's body language so it is not an ideal qualitative methodology.

5

Why are focus groups so popular?

Whilst the traditional stereotypical notion of market research is a large scale quantitative survey, a more modern image might be a group of six to eight mothers sitting on comfy sofas in a living room somewhere in suburbia discussing cooking sauces with a young researcher in his thirties.

The focus group from its early usage in the 1960s has grown and grown and it is now one of if not the most popular tool in market research.

Advantages

Focus groups have perhaps become the most newsworthy of research techniques following their extensive use by political parties in recent years but they do offer a number of advantages over other research methodologies. As discussed earlier (see Chapter 3), they obviously have the benefits of a qualitative approach versus quantitative research methodologies (and the same limitations). However, over and above these generic qualitative research factors, focus groups provide companies with a relatively inexpensive, fast and much more accessible form of knowledge.

Prices for research groups do vary, but at time of going to press a typical group could cost £2,000–£2,500, so a piece of research comprising four groups will cost approximately £10,000. It would probably be completed in four weeks. Four weeks allows a week for recruitment of the agreed sample, a week for conducting the research itself and then two weeks preparing and giving the debrief. On many occasions, this can be compressed – I have done a piece of research like this in a week!

The client (and not necessarily just the market research manager) is involved at all stages. They prepare the brief, choose the agency and then agree the discussion guide, which as the name suggests is an outline that the moderator will use to help him guide the discussion and ensure that all the required topics and issues are covered. Clients can then attend some of the groups. This can be done by either holding one or more of the research sessions in a viewing facility or by a client sitting quietly at the back of the group. (Normally only one 'client' would be allowed to sit in at the back of the group, while most viewing facilities could accommodate eight to ten people viewing the group from behind a one-way mirror.)

By actually viewing some of the groups, clients can gain a good understanding of immediate reactions to any stimulus and hear the real 'consumer' language. Additionally, as communication is much more than simply words, the interpretation of body language and how things are actually said, the tone and intonation, can give rise to further understanding.

Another major advantage is the nature of the debrief. You do not need a maths degree to understand a debrief of a set of focus groups. The results are more often than not in the vernacular, the real language of the consumer. Not surprisingly, quantitative research results contain a lot of numbers – chart after chart of numbers in fact. In contrast, focus-group debriefs are much more discursive and often livened up by the use of the best, sometimes humorous quotes.

The fact that the research is conducted amongst a group of people (normally eight) also brings advantages. It means that it is possible to gain a whole range of different opinions at a single sitting. It can also provide an environment where ideas can be generated, 'sparked' and then built among respondents and so is well suited to creative development work, which can be more difficult to conduct on a one-on-one basis.

Fuelled by market developments

Developments in marketing, and especially in branding, have been a driving force behind the growth of qualitative research and therefore focus groups. One factor fuelling growth has been the spread of the planning cycle. The planning cycle has long been in use in a number of advertising agencies:

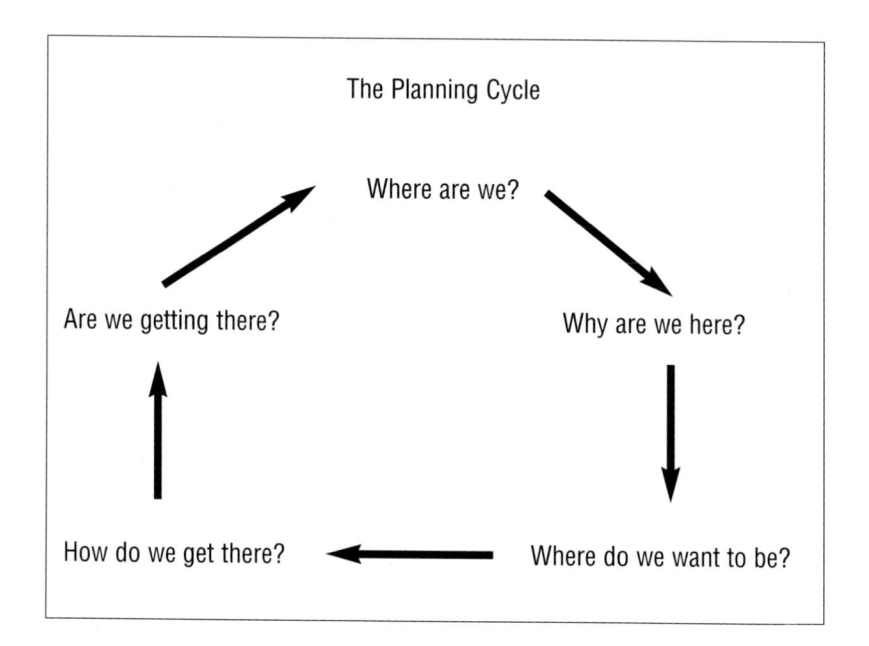

It sets out the stages that an advertising agency should go through in developing advertising and by implication high-lights the need for qualitative research. Across the 1980s and 1990s the spread of the 'planning cycle' or a version of it into marketing disciplines beyond advertising, such as packaging design, corporate identity and new product development, increased the desire for qualitative research and focus groups, in particular as a means of understanding 'why you are where you are' and in helping develop creative work.

A straightforward analogy sometimes used by David Iddiols of HPI relates the planning cycle to the various stages of courtship:

Exploratory	Where am I?	Single
Strategy	Where do I want to be?	Married
Creative	How do I get there?	Send Sarah some flowers and ask her for a date
Evaluative	Am I getting there?	Is Sarah right for me after all?

Source: HPI Research Group

The entrance/growth of new advertisers/brands in sectors such as financial services, IT, telecoms, retail and education that were likely to be very different from the traditional f.m.c.g. (packaged goods) brands and wanted to understand their particular consumer-brand relationships further drove the need for more learning and more focus groups.

Brands and their value to the companies that own them were brought to the fore in 1986 when Nestle bought Rowntree Mackintosh to gain the Rowntree brands. This was one example of the ongoing growing interest and focus on brands. Qualitative research and focus groups in particular are especially useful in understanding brands and brand building.

The rapid growth and increasing dominance of the major supermarket chains has led to an increased emphasis on the search for brand differentiation and new product development as the traditional f.m.c.g. brands struggle to maintain their positions.

As technology has improved and manufacturers can 'copy' each other's improvements, there has also been a shift from purely rational/function-led positionings and propositions to more image- or personality-led positionings. This shift was epitomised in the move from the 'washes whiter' product-led approach of the 1960s to the image-led advertising for lager of the 1980s and 1990s. Just about anything a manufacturer does now can be copied in technical terms by the retailers within months. This emphasis on the more subjective, emotional side of brands puts greater emphasis on understanding people's motivations and needs and their relationship with the brand and therefore stimulates demand for more focus groups.

Growing consumer sophistication is another factor. People are now not just media literate but marketing literate. They have been there, sampled it and bought it all before. Brands, their marketing departments and their agencies desperately want to stay one step ahead.

Not without limitations

All this has meant that focus groups have become increasingly popular and, as mentioned earlier, their use in the political arena has provided them with an even higher profile. However, it is worth noting that there are limitations to the focus-group approach and indeed some practitioners are increasingly worried about this over-reliance on one technique.

Some of the most obvious weaknesses include the negative effect of group dynamics – the way the members of the group interact with each other. In many groups there are a few respondents with strong, even dominant personalities and/or there is an 'expert', or at least someone who believes they are an expert, in the subject. This can dampen other people's responses or even influence them. Minority opinions and attitudes can easily get lost as the less confident individuals choose just to sit there quietly, not wanting to say anything that might appear to conflict with the 'group view'.

Again depending on the personalities of the people in the group it can either put a damper on open and more honest exchange or alternatively encourage some people to lay it on a bit thick. Groups can also have a negative reaction to a particular moderator or the subject, which can seriously reduce the usefulness and/or productivity of a focus-group session.

A particular problem that has also been identified is that of the 'focus groupie' – the professional respondent. Because people are paid to attend these sessions and because it can be easier for recruiters to go back to people they know and have used before, there are a number of instances where some people are being recruited on a very regular basis to attend these sessions. They learn what they think is required of them and then perform accordingly during the group. I once attended groups on two very different subjects at the same venue in subsequent weeks and was a little surprised and annoyed to see two of the same respondents at the second session. Recruiters are normally asked to screen out anyone who has attended a focus group in the last six months.

How a group works

Most if not all groups go through a lifecycle of various stages. These stages were identified and named by W.B. Tuckerman in *Group Work*. The names have stuck – forming, storming, norming, performing and finally mourning.

Forming

Forming is an essential stage in initiating group behaviour where the purpose of the group is explained and the moderator uses various techniques to introduce people to the group and help participants feel at ease so that the group can take on board the task ahead.

There are a number of methods by which the moderator will break the ice. One of the most often used is a paired introduction. After introducing themselves, the moderator puts people into pairs and asks them to find out some details about their partner – their name, how many children they have, whether they work etc. and perhaps something they do in relation to the subject of the group itself, for example do they use cooking sauces? Then the moderator will ask them to introduce their partner to the rest of the group.

These sorts of exercises not only help everyone (including the moderator) learn each other's names, they also ensure each member of the group gets their first opportunity to talk in front of the group. It also encourages people to listen to each other and with prompting from the moderator – 'Does anyone else do that?' – can help start the conversation going.

It is also important at this stage that the moderator establishes that people should talk to the group and not just the moderator. This is usually done with gentle prompting – 'What does everyone think about that?', subtle body language, whereby the moderator does not engage the speaker's eyes, or by shifting their body to include the group.

Storming

This is when a group deals with the distribution of power and finds a way to get on with its task. What happens in many groups is that one or two strong personalities will try to establish their position of 'power' and 'control', their right to lead the group. They may challenge the moderator, raise their voices or use their body language (for example standing up) to (probably subconsciously) convey this 'power'.

This 'storming' can create tension, unease and discomfort in other members of the group, causing them to stop participating. Therefore, moderators try to overcome any problems by:

◆ reminding people that it is fine, even desirable for people to express their own views and disagree
◆ restating the purpose of the group
◆ if necessary, moving on to a new subject.

Norming

This is the stage when a group is unconsciously working out how it will operate in harmony and the nature and depth of communication required. It is when group norms are established. This stage is often used to cover general, non-controversial information, i.e. category, product and brand awareness and usage. As Tuckerman says:

> *When the group has successfully sorted out some of the issues of power and control, it is free to develop trust, cohesion and a degree of intimacy ... group culture emerges. Part of this process is the establishment of norms, or accepted ways of doing things, and agreement about sanctions and where the limits are.*

It is often a fairly short phase before the group really takes off and starts to perform.

Performing

At this stage the group has come together. It is the prime time for tackling the heart of the research and to introduce the more

creative, projective exercises. The moderator will try to maintain this stage for as long as possible, as it is usually the most
productive part of the session. Energy levels tend to be high
and there is often lots of laughter in the group. Moderators
may after a while introduce a new or unexpected technique to
keep those energy levels up.

However, the group can fall out of this mode and back into
a forming mode if dynamics are interrupted. Say, for example,
if the new technique seems less interesting or fun than what
the group had previously been doing. In this case, the moderator must gently get the group back on course and back
performing.

What I am describing here is not a straightforward, linear
process. In many instances storming, norming and performing
will occur a number of times within the course of one focus
group.

Mourning

Sometimes overlooked, the final stage of a group is the mourning. Ideally, the participants should be given time to wind
down and adapt to the end of the group. Good moderators
will signal to the group that the end of the session is approach-
ing. This allows them to consider their views and add anything else they feel is important.

This stage also allows the moderator to thank participants,
reminding them of the purpose of the session, how important
their contributions are and what they might lead to. For example, they might say, 'Keep your eyes open and maybe you'll
see some of the products we've been discussing tonight.'

Most focus groups can stimulate, challenge and provoke;
they are user and participant friendly. They are enjoyable to
participate in, watch and moderate, which might be why they
are so popular. They are perhaps the market research equivalent of reality TV.

6

What are the main techniques of quantitative research?

Perhaps the most famous image of market research is the lady in the street with a clipboard stopping people and asking them a few questions; perhaps the most annoying aspect of market research is the unannounced and badly timed telephone call; and one of the most rapidly growing is the on-line survey. All are examples of the wide variety of quantitative research techniques and data collection methods. The main approaches tend to be based on:

◆ Omnibus surveys (surveys of a representative sample of the population of particular interest)
◆ Ongoing tracking studies (regular repeats of the same survey to monitor trend movement)
◆ *Ad hoc* tailor-made samples and surveys
◆ Econometric modelling (a statistical procedure used to help explain or predict a specific outcome).

The main methodologies include:

◆ Usage and attitudes studies
◆ Segmentation studies
◆ Needs mapping
◆ Product/sensory testing
◆ Packaging testing
◆ Advertising pre-testing
◆ Simulated test markets (STM)
◆ Tracking studies
◆ Brand equity evaluation
    – Advertising and brand tracking
    – Customer satisfaction surveys
    – Retail audits
    – Consumer panels.

(And if this was a more thorough survey of these techniques, not only should these be ranked in order of their usage but their percentage share of the market should be listed as well!)

Usage and attitudes (U&A) studies

U&A studies can be either *ad hoc* or regular surveys to measure and track usage of and attitudes towards the market, brands and products in a defined marketplace. At the beginning of Chapter 3 I set out the sorts of questions you might want to ask if entering the men's toiletries market in the UK. It would include everything from questions about how often men took a shower to whether or not they think Lynx is a modern brand, a brand just for teenagers or a brand that helps make them more attractive to the opposite sex.

Figures from this sort of study probably helped justify the launch of Timotei shampoo in the UK. Many people felt that this brand with its imagery centred on a blonde woman would only appeal to women. However, U&A studies from that time highlighted the changes in men's bathroom behaviour. There was a clear shift from taking baths to everyday showering. Timotei, with its promise of being 'so mild you can wash your hair everyday' and its implied criticism of other harsh shampoos, was the first shampoo to capitalise on this trend and appealed to both men and women.

So it is clear that these sorts of studies are very useful either when a company is considering entering a new marketplace or for tracking comparative performance within a marketplace. They help provide a quantified competitive benchmark of brand performance. In addition, they allow consumer profiling – demographic and potentially psychographic.

Some countries run large-scale annual surveys, which produce a wealth of data on category, brand and media usage, for example the TGI (Target Group Index) survey in the UK.

Needs mapping

It is now increasingly recognised that it is possible to segment people not just by their age, class, sex, life-stage or underlying attitudes, but also by the needs that they have at a certain time or place.

Wendy Gordon was one of the first to define this, explaining the concept as the 'me that I am when' in her MRS conference paper of 1994 entitled 'Retailer Brands':

> *Each person is made up of a number of different people who require a different brand solution in any particular circumstance. Take yoghurt for example. The 'me-that-I-am' when I buy yoghurt for my toddler is different from the me-that-I-am when I buy one for myself as I start to diet. The 'me-that-I-am' when I buy yoghurt depends on different contexts, moods and conditions, each of which may require a different brand solution ...*

Needs mapping is a method aimed at uncovering and understanding the major needs in a given category, i.e. what are the most important physical and emotional needs that the consumers are seeking to meet.

It is normally based on 1,500 to 2,000 consumer interviews, where the consumers indicate which brands and products meet their various needs as described by 300 to 400 different needs statements. These are then correlated, clustered and mapped. The resulting map is used for understanding the needs driving the category, where your brand and your competition's brands sit and what their strengths and weaknesses are. It is, however, important to recognise that this method relies heavily on generating the right needs statements, as well as on the proper statistical analysis and interpretations. Many research companies may deliver different versions of needs-based segmentation. (See Chapter 9 for more on segmentation approaches both quantitative and qualitative.)

Product/sensory testing

Assessments of a product's performance can be conducted 'blind' (without respondents knowing which brand they are trying) or branded. Illogical though it may sound, there are numerous products that perform best in blind tests but which are not the preferred products in branded tests. The 'brand' effect can be significant.

Perhaps the most famous example of this loyalty to a branded (but actually less liked) product is that of New Coke.

In the early 1980s Coca Cola, generally regarded as the world's most valuable brand – according to some surveys Coke was the second most recognised word in the world (after 'ok'), was in trouble. It faced the frightening prospect of losing its number one spot in the American soft drinks market.

Pepsi's aggressive 'Taste challenge' campaign was winning its market share and Coke had to rely increasingly on its dominance in restricted markets such as vending machines and fast food outlets to maintain its market leader position.

Adding to the problem was the success of the brand's stable mate, Diet Coke. As sales of Diet Coke increased and people become converted to the new brand, the pool of available sugar cola drinkers was getting smaller and smaller.

The team in Atlanta embarked on a mission to beat off the Pepsi challenge. Blind taste tests were conducted and showed that people preferred the taste of Pepsi. Based on the results, the management team decided to develop a new Coke. The new formulation they settled on was based on Diet Coke but instead of artificial sweeteners, high fructose corn syrup was added to create a drink that was sweeter and smoother than original Coke – and in fact more like Pepsi.

It is reputed that Coke then undertook the largest ever programme of taste panel research, interviewing over one-quarter of a million people. The results showed that a clear and significant majority of these people preferred the taste of New Coke.

So the question the executives in Atlanta were faced with was should they launch New Coke alongside 'Old' Coke or replace it outright. Worried that if they retained the original alongside the new it might split sales and give the leadership of the sector to Pepsi, they chose to replace the old with the new. The need to maintain secrecy, however, meant that this decision was taken without ever asking the consumers whether they wanted a new, improved Coke. In other words, a branded test was never conducted. On 23 April 1985, New Coke was launched and production of the original formulation was halted later that week.

New Coke proved to be a disaster. America was outraged and by 11 July, senior executives were forced to hold a press conference to announce the return of Classic Coke. Rather than welcoming the better-tasting New Coke, millions of Americans decided they hated it before they tasted it – and even if they did taste it the vast majority convinced themselves they still preferred the original!

Coke was much more to them than just a product; it was an institution, a way of life. It was something they had grown up with, something with which they felt they had a relationship. It was their brand. They reacted with horror and protested long and loud.

Perhaps luckily for Coke, the real surprise was that after the outrage came forgiveness and then celebration at the return of their beloved Classic Coke. So whilst Coke did lose leadership to Pepsi in 1985, Classic Coke, the re-launched original, regained its leadership in 1986 and kept growing. New Coke faded away.

Much sensory testing is also carried out on new products. They are most often tested against brand leaders (if the market/category already exists) whilst product improvements/re-formulations are most often tested against both the competition and the original formulation, which is used as a control. The new product formulation having to demonstrate significant improvement to justify what is normally an increased cost.

Not all sensory testing is done with the consumer. There are in fact four main types of sensory testing panels:

1. *The expert panel* consists of a few extremely well-trained judges with thorough product knowledge. The training period is usually prolonged and the product range for which they are used is relatively limited. Examples would be wine tasters and judges of butter and cheese. An increasing number of research companies have now recruited and offer clients access to specialist 'professional' taste panels. These are used to give insight into brand mapping and/or to provide a useful bridge between consumer comments and product development briefs for technical teams.

2. Perhaps the most widely used panel is the laboratory panel. They can be recruited from company employees (internal panel) or from outside the company (external panel). The most common number of judges is between six and ten. Anyone strongly connected with the production of the product in question is normally avoided since, not surprisingly, they are likely to be prejudiced. People who sit on this type of panel are carefully selected and tested beforehand.

They will undergo a comprehensive training programme for the first few months (often from three to nine months) of their employment. The laboratory panel can be used for most sensory methods with the exception of general preference and acceptance tests where, obviously, consumer panels are used.

3. The third type of panel is the project panel, or the *ad hoc* panel, which consists of a group of people (three to six) who are called together and undergo simple training for a specific project. This type of panel is usually used for simpler tests such as screening tests in selecting products for further testing and/or consumer testing.

4. *The consumer panel* consists of a large number of untrained 'judges' (respondents) who represent a defined consumer group. The samples used can vary from fifty up to several hundred. A larger sample normally (but not always) gives a higher degree of reliability in the analysis of the results.

Packaging testing

Creative development research for packaging is usually conducted qualitatively, but quantitative research is sometimes used to compare and evaluate a new packaging concept against existing packaging and/or its competition. This can be done either using computer-generated images of rows of shelves or indeed re-creating aisles in a venue for respondents to 'shop'. Key factors assessed are normally impact, standout, appeal and communication.

Advertising pre-testing

With the costs of producing commercials often running into hundreds of thousands of pounds and the cost of running them in the millions, pre-testing your commercial to assess its potential to cut-through the others on TV and then actually succeed in getting its message across is increasingly a prerequisite.

Millward Brown is the leading advertising tracking and

pre-testing research company and according to Gordon Brown, one of its founders, advertising works

> *by creating images and associations, which are stored in the memory and then recalled at the point of purchase.*

> *The implications of which are that advertising research should focus on examining the extent to which an ad is able to register the right images and associations in the memory and link them with the right brand.*

Over the many years it has operated in the industry Millward Brown has identified the pre-test measures that it has found to be most closely correlated with 'real life' ad awareness as measured in their tracking studies. These are branding, involvement, appeal and understanding. Their tests deliver an 'awareness index score' – a numeric prediction of on-air performance, which when multiplied by the campaign weight equates to an expected rise in correctly branded prompted awareness. They have also been able to compile a database of norms by sector and by country, against which candidates' ads can be evaluated so that any new ad's likely effectiveness can be compared against its sector's average.

However, the Millward Brown approach is only one of many and as Paul Feldwick of the advertising agency BMPDDB notes:

> *[Pre-testing] is a highly competitive market place, where the suppliers of each technique will tend to stress the merits of their own particular method with a bewildering degree of conviction. The advertiser might well say to himself 'surely they can't all be right?' And his advertising agency may well advise him: 'No, none of them are!'*

Other techniques used in advertising pre-testing include second-by-second measurements, normally done by pressing buttons when the watcher is particularly interested or likes what they see. However, more extreme versions have included measures of eye movement, galvanic skin response and even cerebral activity through electrodes to the head.

The age-old question of whether creativity and research can mix is discussed in a separate, later chapter (see Chapter 16).

Simulated test markets

Simulated test markets (STMs) is a research technique created in the 1960s used to help simulate what might actually happen in a marketplace so that the effect of changes can be predicted. Most often they are used as a method of predicting a volume, or share of market, estimate for a new or re-launched product before it is actually launched.

They have been widely adopted by major manufacturers around the world as an alternative to test marketing, which was slower, more expensive and less secure. Test marketing does have some weaknesses including the fact that it allows competitors to see and even 'steal' your ideas or alternatively competitors can try to sabotage the results.

Based on interviews with consumers, STMs model what a product's sales will be as a function of an estimate of long-term penetration (What percentage of the population tries the product?) and their repeat purchasing (Do they buy the product again and how often do they buy it?), marketplace data and alternative marketing scenarios (including distribution, advertising spends and pricing).

Output from this type of research is normally in the form of a range of estimates reflecting the different marketing scenario inputs (pricing, advertising spend, etc). They therefore provide the marketing team with guidance when setting their budgets and targets. Whilst accuracy is important, it is notoriously difficult given the number of variables that need to be considered. Furthermore, there are concerns that as we move from a mass-marketing approach to a more one-to-one approach, traditional STMs will be less appropriate.

As Joseph Willke, President of AC Nielsen BASES, says in his paper 'The Future of Simulated Test Markets: The Coming Obsolescence of Current Models and the Characteristics of Models of the Future':

> *Current STM models are not well suited for the future marketing world of one-to-one consumer targeting, nor are they well suited for the changing retail environment. They are not well adapted to the increasing granularity with which businesses are managed – at the SKU level, at the individual store level, week by week. As the world changes, all the current forecasting models will begin to break.*

New types will be and are being developed.

Tracking studies

Tracking studies are regular surveys of a defined target audience, most often used (when not a general U&A study) to track advertising and/or brand image.

It is important to remember that whilst advertising awareness is responsive particularly to weight expenditure and good copy, brand attitudes are often much less responsive and therefore generally take longer to respond.

◆ *Advertising and brand tracking* are regular surveys to assess levels of awareness (spontaneous and prompted), claimed usage and attitudes towards brands and their advertising. They can be used to help assess the impact of advertising and other promotional activities. Advertising awareness needs to be measured spontaneously and then prompted to ensure correct recall.

Tracking is then conducted on a number of key criteria as well as on attitude/statements reflecting the desired consumer response to the advertising. Are the consumers getting what we thought we were communicating?

Questions are phrased thus:

'What impression do you get of xxxxx having seen the advertising?'
'I would like you to rate the ad on the following statements using the agree/disagree scale on the card.'

Some studies also ask questions relating to predisposition/closeness to the brand and/or likelihood to purchase.

Many companies that offer pre-testing also offer tracking studies providing both clients and those companies with the information necessary to compare predicted effectiveness with actual effectiveness in the marketplace.

◆ *Customer satisfaction surveys* are often used in service industries and/or for corporate brand surveys of how satisfied customers are with levels of performance/service/value for money.

◆ *Retail audits* are regular audits of retail outlets providing information on the performance of the market, your brand and its competition on such key factors as distribution, sales, pricing and out of stocks.

As originally developed by companies such as AC Nielsen they were designed to give brand owners and managers an objective overview of sales off-take, goods in stock and distribution within different types of retailers (from small independents, cash and carry, multiple chains etc.) and different regions. It allowed management to spot areas of weakness so that action could be taken to rectify any problems, for example large out of stocks, and to assess effects of marketing activity, for example price changes or new advertising. In the past, it was reported every two months.

However, two factors have significantly changed the market for and importance of retail audits. Firstly, the concentration of the grocery trade meant marketers' focus moved from distribution and out of stocks onto the more tactical demands of merchandising, competitive pricing and promotions, for example BOGOFs and three for twos.

Secondly, some of the now much more important major retailers refused to participate if their information was to be separated out, thus downgrading the value of all the information. Consequently consumer panels have become much more important.

EPOS (electronic point of sale) – the scanning of barcodes, which was introduced in the 1980s – has meant that traditional audits have been transformed and now provide much more accurate data more immediately. Weekly reporting is now the norm. With better data, modelling of effectiveness of different marketing activities is also better. The named account problem has not gone away though. Additionally, some retailers now sell their data through brokers.

◆ *Large scale consumer panels* are regular surveys of a panel of consumers to monitor behaviour. They are very useful for assessing usage/consumption of brands and/or media. TNS' Superpanel (which measures household consumption of foods and drink) and the BARB viewing panels (which measure TV consumption) are both good examples.

Omnibus surveys

These are surveys that cover a variety of topics usually because they are funded by a number of different clients, each asking just a limited number of very specific questions – what is the awareness of a particular brand now or what are people's attitudes about a current hot topic?

They are particularly useful because they allow clients to get their answers without the large costs involved in either changing an ongoing tracking study or setting up a completely new study. The samples used tend to be nationally representative and/or composed of people for which there is a general demand.

Econometric modelling

Econometric modelling is a statistical technique normally based on regression that helps provide an explanation of a marketplace outcome (typically an increase or decrease in sales). It requires data from a reasonable period of time covering all the possible factors affecting the outcome (sales), for example economic conditions, distribution, pricing, advertising weight, promotions, weather/temperature and so on.

The data is computer analysed to produce a best-fit model between the outcome and the factors, allowing analysis of which of the factors have the greatest influence. Media planning and buying agencies and other consultancies often use this sort of analysis to try to identify which elements of the marketing mix are most effective for any particular brand.

Initiative, one of the world's leading media agencies, has a dedicated Centre of Excellence – Initiative Consulting – which specialises in this sort of analysis and the chart overleaf shows how this sort of modelling can help 'explain' marketplace performance and then, using the identified coefficients (the multiplier which should be applied to each factor), 'predict' and model future performance.

It is important to remember that any econometric model is unlikely to be definitive; it is the best explanation based on the inputs provided and there will be a proportion of the changes that are the result of unexplained/unknown factors.

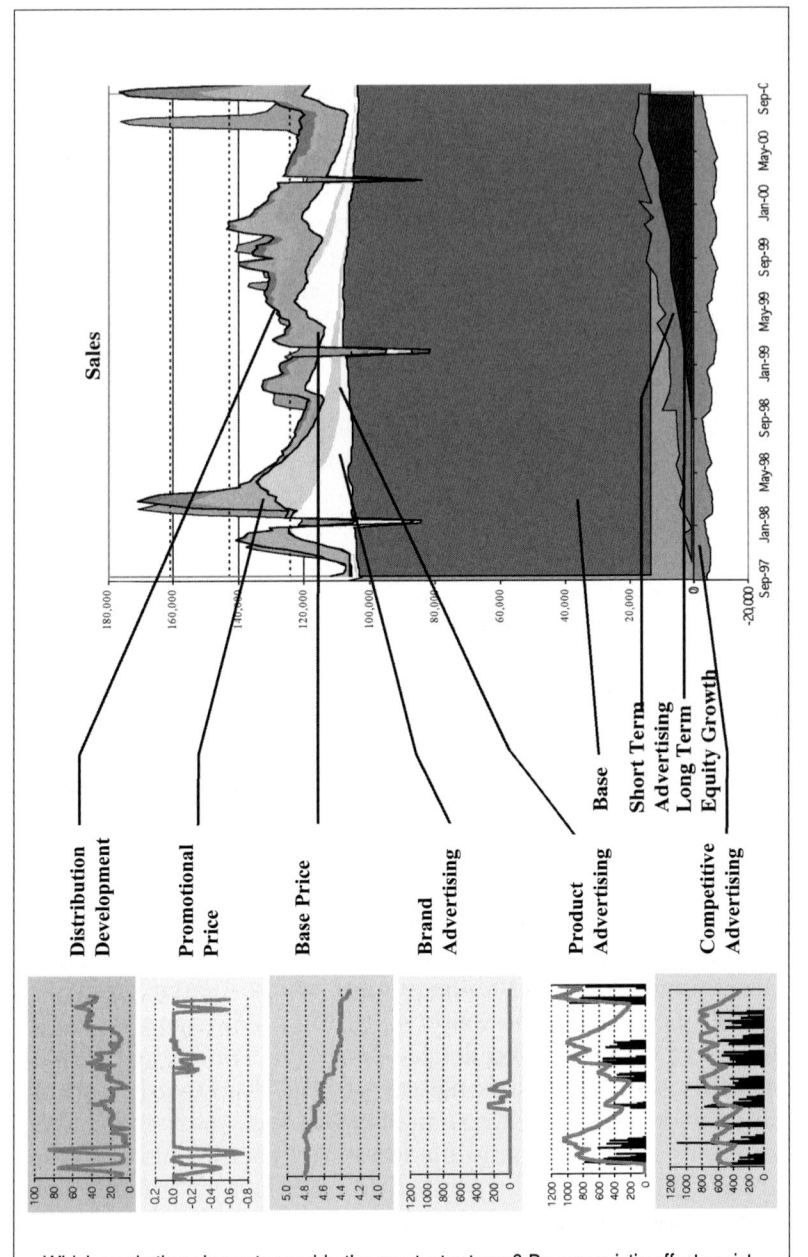

Which marketing elements provide the greatest returns? Do synergistic effects exist between them?
What 'halo' effects exist between different brand's marketing? How can this be leveraged to improve portfolio performance?

Price trade-off models

A price trade-off model is another statistical tool. It aims to model the effects that a change in price has on the volume of sales so that a company can evaluate the impact of any change and plan accordingly. (In economic terms it predicts the price elasticity of demand.)

Brand equity evaluation

Brand equity is an increasingly important business issue. In fact, it has never had such a high profile and is now something that is closely scrutinised when evaluating a company's success. In market research terms it is defined as the 'marketplace value' of the brand, in terms of the strength (and nature) of consumers' relationship with it. Strong brands and strong brand equities are very important assets for any company. Alan Cooper, a partner at HPI, says:

> *A strong equity positively influences a brand's ability to compete successfully, it will help to drive new customer acquisition, generate preference, over and above product or service delivery. It can strengthen existing customer retention and enable a brand to more easily command a premium. It helps underpin successful brand extension and stretch.*

HPI's BrandVitality model is one of a number of approaches to evaluating brand equity. It comprises a series of questions and rating scales that can be asked either as a stand-alone survey or included as part of an ongoing survey – like a tracker. It produces both a single metric of the strength of consumers' relationship with the brand and an array of diagnostics to help explain how the brand's strength is made up.

Only as good as the data itself

Whatever methodology is being used, the validation and reliability of the results will be dependent on a number of factors. One of the most important factors is the collection of the data itself. It is another example of GIGO in research – that is 'garbage in, garbage out'. If the data used is unreliable then the results will be unreliable – it is as simple as that.

All of the methodologies described earlier in this chapter depend to some extent on the collection of the raw data. There are a number of ways in which that data can be obtained but they broadly divide into two categories: interviewing (asking questions) and recording (observation). Within each category, there are a number of specific methodologies.

Interviewing/Asking Questions	Recording/Observation
Postal/self-completion	In person ◆ In-situ ◆ Viewing videos ◆ Garbology
Telephone ◆ Computer-assisted telephone interview (CATI)	Diary
Face to face ◆ Computer-assisted personal interview (CAPI)	Via instruments
Hall test	
Internet	

Each of these categories has different strengths and weaknesses and is more or less appropriate depending on what information is required. Take purchasing of a certain brand of cereal as an example: asking a sample of people whether they have bought that cereal in the last month provides one answer; the survey may also allow you to ask questions about why they bought it and their attitude to it and other brands. However, there may be a very different answer from a retail panel based on surveys of actual sales through a sample of stores. Whilst the retail panel is likely to provide a more accurate answer to what was actually sold, where and for how much, it cannot provide a profile of those who bought it. An in-home consumer panel, which monitors actual consumption, will tell you the profile of users and how much/how often they have used it.

It is always important to recognise the difference in actual or claimed behaviour (attitudes) that is being considered. My late father, who was a statistician, always stressed the limitations of claimed behaviour or, in this case, ownership rather than actual. He told the story of a census interview in Africa where a farmer was asked how many cows, sheep and goats he owned. He answered 'None' and yet the interviewer could plainly see a number of goats in the man's house and a few cows and sheep in the yard. When asked to whom these animals belonged the man claimed that they were his neighbour's. The man being interviewed did not want to be known as owning anything he might be taxed on. My father recommended that the interviewers counted the animals and recorded those figures!

This is one of the most fundamental issues that needs to borne in mind when reviewing quantitative research. (See the appendix for the other important questions you should always ask.)

Interviews and other means of asking questions

There are a number of ways in which questions/interviews can be asked/conducted for quantitative research.

◆ *By post*: Postal surveys can be very cost-effective (you don't need a fieldwork team) and can provide a possible tool for PR at the same time, but they have a slow turnaround time and a self-selecting sample.

◆ *By telephone*: Telephone surveys are useful with data-based samples and business samples for short interviews. However, they cannot be used where stimulus material needs to be shown to respondents. They also have perhaps the worst reputation amongst the general public, as telesales sometimes pretend to be conducting research as a means to start a conversation – sales pitch.

◆ *Face to face*: Face-to-face interviews can be either in the home, in the workplace or on the street and allow for stimulus materials. Home-based interviewing provides scope for longer interviews. However, they are not effective for low-penetration markets/brands, as you will have to ring on a lot of bells before you find someone who uses the product and is willing to be interviewed! Computer-assisted methods are increasingly being used and can be very useful where there is complicated routing of the interview or multi-media stimulus.

◆ *Hall test*: Research conducted in halls (community halls, council buildings, church halls etc.) provides many of the benefits of a face-to-face interview but does so in a more controlled environment. This enables a marketing team to attend and watch some interviews being conducted. It often facilitates faster turnaround of results. However, it is better suited to shorter interviews.

◆ *Via the internet*: Research via the internet is rapidly growing on the back of internet penetration and the fact that they are highly cost-effective. In fact, it is estimated (by Harris Interactive) that in the US between 40 and 50 per cent of all custom revenues will be for on-line research by 2005. Another agency, Inside Research, estimates that 24 per cent of US agency survey revenue will come from on-line research. However, in the UK and Europe, revenue from on-line research is a lot less; estimates for 2003 are only 3–5 per cent, though rising rapidly to between 15 and 20 per cent by 2005.

Some of the undoubted appeal is that turn-around times (the time from commissioning to reporting) can be very fast, as responses tend to be more immediate. Most people who are going to respond do so within 48 hours.

Internet research also allows for the inclusion and presentation of images/pictures/mock-ups, which the more traditional telephone surveys cannot handle. However, there are some limitations; in particular there are issues with self-selecting samples.

Recording/observation

Similarly there are a number of ways in which data can be recorded or observed for quantitative studies:

◆ *In person*: Generally an accurate means of data but can be very costly and time consuming. If it involves the analysis of recorded behaviour it may be open to more subjective personal interpretation.

◆ *Diary*: Asking panels to keep a diary is a good methodology for long-term tracking of behaviour in-home – purchasing, usage, media consumption. However, it is dependent on rigorous completion and therefore always liable to some margin of error. Increasingly, technology is being used to replace or at least supplement this sort of data collection.

◆ *Via instruments*: The use of specific instruments to measure behaviour is in principle the most accurate and rigorous, but it can be limited in situations where the survey participants themselves operate the instruments.

Other sources of quantitative research

It is also important to remember that there are other widely available sources of quantitative data, which include company-specific data and statistics published by the government and other institutions.

Company data: This is data collected by the company, which, if analysed and applied, can provide key marketing intelligence. The information includes ex-factory sales data, response levels to promotions and customer lists.

Government statistics and other published data: Much of this information (especially that collected and published by the government) can be classified as either social or economic research but also provides important information and insights for the marketer. For example, the CSO Social Trends information provides important demographic, economic and social information.

> *It draws together statistics from a wide range of government and other organisations to paint a broad picture of British society today, and how it is changing.*

So whilst you will find statistics on demographics, income and employment, you could also find out the level and trends in breastfeeding by social class, offenders as a percentage of the total population, water quality in rivers and canals, the distance travelled on foot by different age groups and much more. This publicly available data can be broadly split into (i) more general sources for information on the macro-environment and (ii) more specific trade-related information sources.

There is a range of information published by the government, other international bodies (UN, OECD), academic institutions and the general media, which can provide information on the economy, population and social trends. More specialised information on a number of sectors is available via trade bodies and the associated trade press. It is also possible to gain information on other companies (competitors) from their company reports. Information like this can of course be supplemented by retail visits, product purchases and feedback from your own sales and technical people.

7

What is statistical significance?
(And is it significant?)

Y ou do not need to understand how a television works, let alone be able to build or mend one to enjoy the pro- grammes shown on it; you do need to know how to turn it on, how to change channels and where to find a repair- man if you require one. The same is basically true about quan- titative market research. You do not need to know all the statistical theory behind sampling and significance testing to use quantitative research, but it is useful to know why they are important, what are some of the issues you should be aware of and where to find a good quantitative research agency if you need one.

So, if you were about to skip reading this chapter, please stop, think again and give the chapter a chance. My aim with this book is to provide an easy-to-read introduction to market research. Now, I cannot do that without discussing sampling and statistical significance, but I do not intend to go into the theory and proofs behind them.

If after all this you are still interested in learning more about the subject, then there are a number of good books whose authors can explain it much better than I ever could. I have included a list of a few at the end of the chapter. There is also the MRS as well as a lot of good quantitative research agencies that have people who do this for a living and I know that they would be happy to explain it to you.

Here's a whistle-stop introduction to sampling, statistical theory and statistical differences. Sampling is fundamental to quantitative research because almost all market research is conducted using a sample of some sort. Most quantitative research is used to understand and measure things amongst large samples or 'populations' of people, indeed it may often be the total population of a country that is under investigation. However, it would be very impractical, extremely time-consuming and incredibly expensive, not to mention boring for the participants, if every bit of market research was conducted amongst the total target group. So, instead, samples are used. An analogy would be governing a country. If everyone had to vote on everything it would be time-consuming, expensive and impractical which is why we have a government, which is a sample of the total adult population.

However, before going on to samples, it is important to recognise the importance of defining the population from which the sample is to be taken, as all results will obviously relate back to that defined population and careful definition is essential. For example, are we interested in the views of buyers or those of users of a specific brand? These two 'populations' are often far from being identical groups: just think about nappies – buyers and users are very different. A basic definition of a sample is set out by Paul Harris in 'Sampling and Statistics':

A sample is selected from a population to give representative and unbiased data from that population.

In other words, a sample is a subset of a total population from whom any results should *broadly* be the same as those that would have been obtained if the whole of that population had been surveyed. (This may be where my analogy with parliament breaks down!) The key word is broadly. What this means is that in any one specific case the sample might over- or under-represent what the total population would say but in the long run, if you averaged a number of surveys, the results would equal that of the entire population.

However, 'broadly' is not good enough for most market research. A 'good' sample design should give a true result most of the time with only small differences – or as statisticians might say, margins of error or sampling errors. Furthermore, for most market research it is possible to calculate the likely size and scale of these errors as they depend on both the size of the sample and the sample design.

The two main methods of sampling used in market research are *random sampling*, which is where the sample is drawn by some chance process, and *quota sampling*, where the researcher selects certain characteristics (age, gender, socioeconomic etc.) and sets out quotas (set numbers/proportions) for each of them. These quotas (and how they interlock and overlap) then form the basis for selecting interviewees. The main advantage of quota sampling is its cost and speed. Harris estimates:

> *It can be up to half the cost of a random sample of the same size.*

This is because quota samples are quicker and easier to undertake than random samples.

As mentioned earlier, it is possible using statistical theory to estimate the size and scale of the likely margins of error – the possible variations in results. The margins of error depend on both the size and design of the sample. How this is calculated and why you can rely on it is all to do with sampling distribution, normal distribution and standard errors – none of which I plan to go into here.

However, they all become particularly important when it comes to comparing results in any research. Say we have conducted two surveys in consecutive years, each of 2,000 adults, to identify the number of people who drink wine.

◆ In 2001, 51.2 per cent of the sample said they drink wine nowadays.
◆ In 2002, 52.7 per cent of the sample said they drink wine nowadays.

The difference is an increase of 1.5 per cent. Is this a valid difference or just a sampling error? Do more people drink wine nowadays? What, if any, degree of certainty can we have that the difference is 'real'?

Luckily, or cleverly, for quantitative research it is possible, as mentioned earlier, that if you know the sample size and its design you can work out, using a (complex) equation, whether any difference is statistically significant at a given confidence level.

How confident? Well most research will look at defining whether or not any differences are significant at either a 95 per cent or 99 per cent level. In other words, if we are using 99 per cent significance levels and the difference is statistically significant you can be 99 per cent sure that the difference is 'real'. This process is more formally described by Harris:

*The statistical method for objectively deciding whether a dif-
ference is real or not can be explained by sampling variation.
When the observed difference between the two percentages is
greater than a certain margin, then we say that the difference
is statistically significant and we can conclude that a real
change … has taken place.*

It is also possible to compare results within the survey, comparing, for example, the number of 25 to 34 year olds who
claim they drink wine with the number of 35 to 44 year olds
who drink and again we can identify whether any differences
are statistically significant.

---

*Further and more detailed reading can be found in the list below. A more
simplified list of the sorts of questions to ask when presented with any
piece of quantitative research is included in the appendix.*

Harris, P. 'Sampling and Statistics' in Robin Brin, Paul Hague and Phyllis
Vangelder (eds) *A Handbook of Market Research Techniques*, Kogan Page,
1990

Cochran, William, G. *Sampling Techniques*, Wiley, 1965

Kish, L. *Survey Sampling*, Wiley Classics Library, John Wiley & Sons,
1995

8

How should you ask a question?

Asking the Embarrassing Question
by Allen H. Barton, University of Chicago

The pollster's greatest ingenuity has been devoted to finding ways to ask embarrassing questions in non-embarrassing ways. We give here examples of a number of techniques, as applied to the question: 'Did you kill your wife?'

1. *The casual approach*
   Do you happen to have murdered your wife?

2. *The numbered card*
   Would you please read off the number on this card which corresponds to what become of your wife? (Hand card to respondent)
   1. Natural death
   2. I killed her
   3. Other (What?)
   (Get card back from respondent before proceeding)

3. *The 'everybody' approach*
   As you know, many people have been killing their wives these days. Do you happen to have killed yours?

4. *The 'other people' approach*
   a) Do you know any people who have murdered their wives?
   b) How about yourself?

5. *The sealed ballot technique*
   In this version you explain that the survey respects people's rights to anonymity in respect to their marital relations and they, themselves, fill out the answer to the question, seal it in an envelope and drop it in a box conspicuously labelled 'sealed ballot box' carried by the interviewer.

6. *The projective technique*
   What thoughts come to mind as you look at the following
   pictures?
   (Note: The relevant responses will be evinced by picture D)

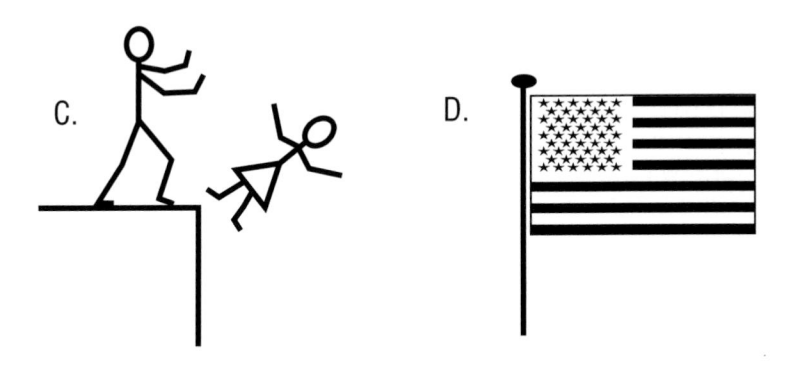

7. *The Kinsey Technique*
   Stare firmly into the respondent's eyes and ask in simple
   clear-cut language such as that to which the respondent is
   accustomed and with an air of assuming that everyone has
   done everything:
   Did you ever kill your wife?

8. *Putting the question at the end of the interview.*

This humorous take on asking questions appeared in
Commentary in spring 1962. (*Commentary* was later renamed

The Journal of the Market Research Society). It builds on the old favourite, 'Have you stopped beating your wife yet?', which is probably the most famous example of another variation on question asking – *the assumed guilty approach* – whereby the question is framed on the assumption that the respondents have definitely done what you are asking them about and you are now ascertaining more information.

Questions – an open and closed case

One of the important distinctions concerning questions in market research is the difference between open (or open-ended) questions and closed questions.

Closed

Broadly defined, a closed question is one that can be answered simply and definitively, often with just one word or phrase (though not necessarily just yes or no). For example, 'How old are you?' is a classic closed question. Closed questions also include multiple-choice-type questions, whereby people are given a number of answers from which they need to choose one, even if that one is 'Don't know'.

Closed questions have the following characteristics:

◆ They give you *facts*
◆ They are easy to answer
◆ They are quick to answer
◆ They keep control of the conversation with the questioner.

As such, closed questions are very useful and important in quantitative research when you have limited time to get through a series of questions and you want to be able to easily assess and categorise the answers.

Examples of closed questions for market research include:

◆ Have you ever bought whiskey?
◆ Do you like whiskey?
◆ How often do you drink whiskey?

There are some potential drawbacks in the use of closed questions. These include situations where badly formed or non-tested questions are used and so do not anticipate answers or do not allow likely honest answers (and you get back to 'Have you stopped beating your wife?' again).

Open

Open questions are, as the name suggests, those that aim to open up a conversation or discussion. Generally they cannot be answered by a single word or phrase; they are an invitation for people to talk, to volunteer new information, to tell you their views or feelings.

Open questions have the following characteristics:

◆ They ask the respondent to think and reflect
◆ They will give you *opinions* and *feelings*
◆ They hand control of the conversation to the respondent.

As such they are the basis of much qualitative research where the objective is to get people to talk, to give detailed information and to explain what they do, think and feel and why.

Examples of open questions are:

◆ Why do you think whiskey is your favourite spirit?
◆ How does drinking whiskey compare with drinking other spirits?
◆ How would you describe drinking whiskey to someone who has never drunk it?

Projective questions as discussed in Chapter 8 are most likely to be open-ended questions:

◆ If whiskey were a person, what sort of person would they be?

Open-ended questions can and often are used in quantitative research too. The results are then reviewed and where possible put into clusters of similar responses (even if the exact language/phrasing is different). Results can then be presented in a similar form to the rest of the quantitative survey. So, for example, an open-ended question on a quantitative survey might be:

◆ Why do you like whiskey?

This allows respondents to answer in any way they like and to offer as much or as little information but (hypothetically) the answers might then be categorised as follows:

(Any mention) Taste	52%
Smooth	35%
Fiery	23%
Peaty	10%
Taste (unspecified)	8%
(Any mention) Alcoholic	21%
Strong/powerful	10%
Makes me drunk	6%
Good mixed with other drinks	5%
Other	12%

Whose side are you on?

Another important distinction is that between neutral and leading questions. Neutral questions are non-judgemental and do not reveal or reflect any particular perspective or view. Leading questions are those that reveal the views (or bias) of the questioner and/or try to direct the respondent to one answer.

A key issue in research is therefore the need to use neutral questions so as not to lead or direct responses. If a moderator suggests they particularly like or dislike something it may bias the response of the group or person they are interviewing and as we have seen from the questionnaire in the article in *Commentary* it is possible to construct leading questions in quantitative research.

One recent and very topical example came to light on 10 December 2003, when the government published a bill that announced the wording for the question in a possible referendum on the choice of the future currency for the UK. The exact wording would be:

Should the United Kingdom adopt the euro as its currency?

This question was always going to be one of the controversial questions of the year, given the intense political debate on the euro, and was bound to have its critics. Alan Duncan, the Conservative Party's spokesman on constitutional affairs, claimed in the *Metro* that:

> *The proposed referendum question breaches Electoral Commission guidelines on fair wording. It makes no mention that the pound would be replaced if people voted 'yes'.*

Matthew McGregor, campaign manager of the anti-euro campaign, also expressed concerns, saying:

> *We would argue that 'adopt' is pretty positive sounding.*

Both might prefer a question along the lines of:

> *Do you want to replace the pound as the official currency of Great Britain and use the euro instead?*

But Dr Cillian Ryan, a political expert from the University of Birmingham, when asked said the question seemed neutral but went on to the crux of the matter:

> *The question is fine but whether Mr Brown gets the answer he is after is another matter.*

Primary and secondary questions and the case for a second 'why?'

Market research is all about asking questions and in many instances it pays to take a leaf out of the world's best question masters – four-year-old children. As any parent knows they rarely if ever are satisfied with asking 'Why?' just once. They ask it again and again ... and again. So whilst we all use primary questions to introduce a topic and secondary questions to probe for more information, in qualitative research it is useful to go on to tertiary questions and beyond.

Experience has shown that often people stop when they get

to one 'sensible' answer, a good answer to the first 'Why?' Not enough people ask the second 'Why?' One example of this in action concerns shampoos-and-conditioners-in-one. When they were first researched people asked 'Why?' and not liking the answer rejected the idea. They felt a product could not wash OUT the dirt whilst simultaneously putting IN the conditioner. However, when P&G positioned Wash'n'Go as 'the most convenient way to wash your hair' this overcame the problem. People asked 'Why?' and were given the perfectly 'sensible' answer of because it is a shampoo and conditioner in one. As the success of its launch showed, many people were clearly satisfied after their first 'Why?' was satisfactorily answered.

Good qualitative researchers are therefore like four-year-old children and will ask the second and third 'Why?' However, the real skill is in making these probing questions non-judgemental or non-threatening. There is an art to asking the same question repeatedly and to asking more probing questions without annoying or embarrassing the respondent.

Order effect

It is a well-proven fact that the order in which we are asked a set of questions can considerably affect our answers. There has been a great deal of research into this phenomenon. A simple but telling example is quoted below from *Michigan Today Online*, fall 2001, where Norbert Schwarz, Professor of Psychology, describes his favourite example:

> We did a study where we asked students, 'How satisfied are you with your life? How often do you have a date?' The two answers were not statistically related – you would conclude that there is no relationship between dating frequency and life satisfaction. But when we reversed the order and asked, 'How often do you have a date? How satisfied are you with your life?' the statistical relationship was a strong one. You would now conclude that there is nothing as important in a student's life as dating frequency.
>
> This is an example of a question-order effect – which is just one of many ways that survey questions can affect the answers we receive. Most questions do not influence one another. But when questions are substantively related, then question-order

effects like this one are among the most stable and reliable find-ings in the survey research literature.

This effect is often referred to as 'priming', i.e. the use of certain questions in a specific order leads or 'primes' the respondent to be more or less likely to give a certain answer. In the example above asking the question about the frequency of dating first primes the respondent about their views on satisfaction with life. It is possible to test for priming effects by having questions in different orders in different versions of a questionnaire, randomly assigning respondents to these different versions and then using statistical procedures to compare responses for the different versions.

9

Do they mean us?
How and why does research help
segment the population?

T-Mobile the telecoms company was formerly known as One-2-One, which was formerly known as Mercury. As the company evolved it commissioned HPI to undertake some research amongst its employees to help develop the most productive workplace culture. During the process, David Iddiols became increasingly aware that he could neatly divide the workforce into three distinct groups

1. Creators – who had lots of ideas
2. Critics – who panned most of those ideas
3. Careful – who rarely ventured an opinion.

It was a segmentation that would help them develop strategies for each type.

Phil Spires is a friend of mine who is an associate director at the research agency Vegas. He is also a DJ with Soxan, a network of DJs and video artists set up for those who couldn't attend the Big Chill in Naxos in 2001. If you press him he will divide the whole world into three basic types – what he calls '*the 3Ds*':

> *Those who **D**ance*
> *Those who **D**on't dance*
> *And those who **DJ***

It is a simple and memorable segmentation that for him helps not only categorise the population but identify his target audience (those who will dance) and his potential allies / competitors (other DJs) more clearly.

It is an age-old truism that you cannot be everything to

everyone all the time. Companies and brands need to focus. They need to decide on whom they should concentrate their resources, whose needs they want to try to satisfy, who they wish to contact/communicate with.

Whilst there are a number of factors such as the advance of technology and a growing demand for individuality that are facilitating more one-to-one or customised marketing approaches, the norm for most brands and most markets is still mass marketing. Mass marketing is based on a company/brand satisfying the needs of a group of people.

To do this as successfully as possible it is important for brands to segment the population in some way so as to identify the specific groups of people with whom they will do most business. Once they know who these people are and what it is that makes them similar then it is easier for them to get to understand them and their specific needs better. It allows them to target their communication better and more cost-effectively; to understand what sort of messages and what sort of media they respond better to; and to identify opportunities for product improvements and new product and service development.

Segmentation is therefore an important tool in developing any marketing strategy and a key use for market research. There are a huge range of segmentations and approaches from simply dividing the population into men and women to more qualitative segmentations based on attitudes and lifestyles.

Basic demographic segmentation

Perhaps the simplest and, still, the most often used segmentations are the basic demographic segmentations of age and gender. Whilst more sophisticated segmentations are available it is still important for marketers to know if their basic target group is predominately men aged 18 to 25, women aged 25 to 44 or babies under 2 years. Demographic statistics are collated and provided by most governments.

Class or socio-economic segmentation

After basic demographic segmentation perhaps the most utilised approach is that which uses social class (or more correctly occupation) as the distinguishing variable. It is used by the NRS (the National Readership Survey), many if not most other media bodies and widely within the market research fraternity. This is despite the government's repeated assertion that we are no longer a class-driven society and numerous statements from various marketing practitioners that a class- or occupation-driven segmentation is out of date.

There are six categories: A, B, C1, C2, D and E:

◆ *A*s are professional people, comprising very senior managers in business or commerce or top-level civil servants. They account for only 3 per cent of the population. They include retired people who were previously grade A and their widows.

◆ *B*s are approximately 20 per cent of the population. They are middle management executives in large organisations, principal officers in local government and the civil service. They are top managers in small business concerns, education and service establishments. They include retired people who were previously grade B and their widows.

◆ *C1*s are approximately 28 per cent of the population. They are junior management and/or owners of small establishments and all others in non-manual positions – a very varied assortment of jobs. They also include retired people who were previously grade C1 and their widows.

◆ *C2*s are all skilled manual workers and those manual workers with responsibility for other people. They include retired people who were previously grade A and their widows if receiving pensions from their late husband's job. They account for around 21 per cent of the population.

◆ *D*s account for about 18 per cent of the population and are all semi-skilled and unskilled manual workers, apprentices and trainees. They include retired people previously grade D with pensions from their job.

◆ *E*s account for 10 per cent or so of the population and include all those entirely dependent on the state long term, due to old age, unemployment, sickness or other reasons.

They also include those unemployed for a period exceeding six months, casual workers and those without a regular income.

The categories can be further divided into seventeen groups if required.

Regional/geographical

Another obvious means of segmenting the population is on the basis of where they live – by county or state, depending on what country you are considering. CACI's ACORN tool is a geo-demographical approach which segments the UK's residential postcodes into demographic and lifestyle types. The latest version of ACORN, launched in 2003 and based on the 2001 census, categorises all 1.9 million UK postcodes using over 100 demographic statistics and over 250 lifestyle variables and classifying the population into five key categories:

1. Affluent achievers
2. Urban prosperity
3. Comfortably well-off
4. Modest means
5. Hard pressed

These in turn break down into 17 groups, such as 'Flourishing Families' in the affluent achievers category and 'Prosperous Professionals' in the urban prosperity category, creating a total of 56 consumer types. John Rae, Director of Business Development at CACI, said:

> *People in similar areas tend to have similar needs and aspirations and make similar lifestyle choices. Without knowing who they are, ACORN's sophisticated classification allows us to find these people, and predict how much they will spend, and on what products.*

ACORN is widely used to help target direct marketing and advertising campaigns, to aid companies, retail outlets and public services in the location when making decisions.

Attitudinal acronyms

Using quantitative cluster analysis or a more subjective qualitative approach, it is possible to identify segments of the population who are unified by their attitudes, beliefs and behaviour.
It has become the vogue to christen the different segments that
have been identified with light-hearted but memorable names
such as The Merry Wives of Windsor.

One approach to generating these names is to use acronyms
to name the different segments: the Y-UP-Pies (Young
Upwardly-mobile Professionals) are perhaps the most famous;
DINKies are Double Income No Kids; whilst LOMBARD
stands for Lots Of Money But A Real Dickhead.

Girls, lads, men and rangers

Mainstream media picked up on this sort of segmentation and
helped popularise the approach starting with The Sloane
Ranger. Researcher Peter York in his analysis of the 1980s identified a certain type/new breed of young women: the Sloane
Ranger. The name combined a reference to Sloane Square, the
natural habitat of the breed, and played off the name Lone
Ranger. It has often been said that Princess Diana, before her
marriage to Prince Charles, was the archetypal Sloane Ranger.

It wasn't long before her antithesis, the white stiletto-wear-
ing, dancing round her handbag Essex Girl, was born and also
became a favourite of the tabloids.

The men struck back and in the 1990s. Men who wanted to
be one of the boys, who despite women's lib, still revelled in
boys' things (football, films and women in sexy lingerie), acted
like big kids and read new magazines like *Loaded* were christened 'New Lads'.

Perhaps not surprisingly 'New Ladettes' soon followed, but
they weren't the only sequel. Following in their southern
cousins' stilettos come Chessex Girls – a wealthier, 'Cheshire',
flashier (bling, bling) equivalent of the old Essex Girl.

Brandographics

As Sir Michael Perry, ex-Chairman of Unilever, said we are

increasingly defined not by who we are but what we buy. As he said in a speech to the Marketing Society in 1994:

> *In the modern world, brands are a key part of how individuals define themselves and their relationships with one another ... More and more we are simply consumers ... We are what we wear, what we eat, what we drive.*

So after demographics and psychographics, we now have brandographics. Because the best brands are ubiquitous and the images and associations of them are broadly held, they are another means by which people can be segmented.

Hence in the 1997 election, the key segment that the Labour Party's researchers identified was christened 'Mondeo Man'.

A segmentation of qualitative researchers

A few years ago I decided that it was about time to do unto researchers what they do to us and created an informal segmentation of qualitative researchers. Published in *Marketing* magazine the segments included:

> *The Psychobabbler: Closest to an academic or at least likes to think so. Interested in the latest developments in semiotics or psychology, his/her aim is to make the difficult and complex simple and understandable. In reality, their debriefs succeed in making the simple and understandable difficult and complex.*

> *The Smooth Operator: Usually male, they seduce consumers by hinting at their need to be mothered or mildly flirting with the group. Especially suited to mainstream research amongst bored housewives.*

The other groups were The School Ma'am, Bearded of Islington, The Empathiser and Too Cheerful to Be True. (And if you ever meet me you can see if you can tell which one I am!)

10

Can market research predict the future?

A t the general election of 1992, right up until the actual results were announced, the opinion polls were predicting a victory for Neil Kinnock and the Labour party. Yet it would be another five years before Labour would win a general election and the new Prime Minister would be Tony Blair and not Neil Kinnock.

In hindsight some commentators have argued that Neil Kinnock's overly triumphant tone in those last few days, when he thought he had won, in fact swung voters away from him and thus the election was lost. If this were true (though it is only one of many theories) then the market research might have been proved right had it not been made public and had not Labour believed it.

Neil Kinnock and Tony Blair

Whatever the truth of the matter, it is a famous case of how research cannot be relied upon to predict the future accurately. There are many other commentators who would endorse this view. Anita Roddick, founder of The Bodyshop, said:

> *You can't tell much about what's coming from looking in the rear view mirror of market research.*

And even that famous 'researcher' Sherlock Holmes said:

The past and the present are within the field of my inquiry, but what a man may do in the future is a hard question to answer.

However, Watts Wacker and Jim Taylor in *The 500-Year Delta* suggest that there is a way of successfully predicting the future and then putting any plan in action:

Challenges arrive sequentially. Information is gathered. Wise heads are consulted. A plan is formed. Contingencies are pondered and provided for. Ducks are lined up. The big guns are pulled out. And finally the solution is executed.

But as they go on to say this only ever happens

in storybooks – and undoubtedly still in some graduate courses in basic management practices.

There are a number of reasons why predicting the future is so difficult. The first and most obvious is that the future has not yet happened so there is nothing to measure or assess. This means everything has to be based on what people say they will do or extrapolating from past behaviour, neither of which delivers certainty, as the Neil Kinnock example clearly demonstrates. When asked in numerous opinion polls, people had said they were going to vote Labour but when the time came not all of those who said they were going to actually did. Asking people what they do or what they will do is never as accurate as measuring what they actually do. In short, predictive data is never as reliable as performance data. People claim to eat a lot more brown and wholemeal bread than they actually do.

Asking what they want does not always work either. It is often said that if Henry Ford had asked people what they wanted they would have said a faster horse. As Tim Ambler of the London Business School has said:

Nearly every famous innovation has nothing to do with focus groups. Anything truly innovative runs counter to accepted conventions.

Additionally, when asking about the future, people are often responding to new ideas and concepts.

One imagines that a focus group would very likely have turned down the Great Pyramid (impractical), Beethoven's late quartets (too difficult) and Picasso's Guernica (too inflammatory). The Egyptians, Beethoven and Picasso were all prepared to think the unthinkable. That's the nature of creativity and we are all very grateful they were so pig-headedly unreasonable. Alas we live in a culture that encourages feeble-minded political correctness supported by bogus research.

Stephen Bayley in *Labour Camp: The Failure of Style over Substance* suggests that it is all too easy to reject the new. Further, the 'new' marketing concepts may not be fully realised in the stimulus materials with which they are presented. This in turn means people's claimed 'expected' response may actually be very different when they find themselves faced with the real thing. They may like the idea as it is expressed as a concept but then dislike the final execution. They may not understand the stimulus but might actually have liked the product if it was made and presented to them.

Seeing a storyboard or an animatic (a simple animated storyboard) of a planned new TV commercial can be very different from seeing the real thing and so the responses could be very different. (See the Heineken example quoted in Chapter 13.) Having a product described to you is very different from feeling, smelling or tasting the actual final product. Prototypes can sometimes help overcome this sort of problem. However, this is not always the case. I have been involved in research where bench (short-run, hand-produced) samples were tested and loved by people and yet final production-line-produced products were different and not liked nearly as much. Not surprisingly, the product failed in the marketplace.

Many new product ideas do very well in the early stages of research and are therefore predicted to do well in the marketplace. However, many new products fail every year – even if it is not quite the apocryphal nine out of ten.

Despite these issues, there are a number of ways in which market research or research techniques are used to 'predict' the future.

Spotting trends

Trend spotting can be divided into two approaches along a broadly qualitative/quantitative axis.

Hard

'Hard' trend spotting is usually undertaken by more formal bodies and institutes. They use a variety of different quantitative sources of 'historical' information to identify trends and so predict future developments. These bodies come in all shapes and sizes from think-tanks such as the 'Institute for Public Policy Research' to the more specialised and topic-specific institutes such as 'The Army Environmental Policy Institute'.

More obvious trends that can be identified and predicted include shifts in demographic profiles. Whilst these are very useful in their own right, the potential nuances and implications of these sorts of trends may still need to be determined.

Take for example the current trend in the UK towards an ageing population. This is undisputed information based on census data. Whilst in marketing terms this suggests the possible growth of products aimed at older people, for example Saga holidays, it is the identification of such softer or 'sub' trends as more 'active grandparents' (instead of watching their grandchildren on a roller-coaster they are right there sitting beside them) and the emergence of 'silver surfers' (the burgeoning number of older users on the web) that is likely to drive more productive marketing solutions.

Soft

'Soft' trend spotting – futurology as it is increasingly called – is a more subjective and qualitative approach. It is about spotting shapes and patterns in modern culture, consumer behaviour and different marketplaces. Wendy Gordon in *Good Thinking* suggests that being a good trend spotter

> ... *requires a certain amount of sensitivity, awareness and synthesis across a range of studies in different product and service categories.*

One trend I have observed is that there is a growth in soft-trend spotting. There is an increasing number of people offering their services as futurologists, including the management and business gurus and the more specialised 'cool sleuths' who seek out the latest trends amongst the young and leading-edge groups of society. Many go on to write books on the subject. In addition a number of major companies have appointed their own futurologists.

As I'm writing this section on predicting the future (October 2003), another report on what life might be like in future has just been published. It comes from the UK Environment Agency and specifically looks at what life might be like in 2020. So just in case you are reading this in 2020 and want proof that research can (or cannot) predict the future here are ten predictions from that report about the family and their house of the future:

♦ *Power*: Household windmill and solar panel generate surplus electricity to feed back into the national grid providing a small income.
♦ *Pollution*: Meter checks whether the family has exceeded its greenhouse gas allowance.
♦ *Health*: Toilet automatically analyses samples and digitally sends the information to doctor's surgery.
♦ *Children*: Often adopted because chemicals have caused low sperm count and infertility in many men.
♦ *Water*: Families have their own purification plants for recycling toilet and household waste.
♦ *Groceries/food*: 'Smart' fridge automatically orders bread, milk, yoghurt and other produce as the family runs short. The family keeps its own chickens for eggs.
♦ *Communication*: Phones powered by electricity generated in people's brains.
♦ *Transport*: Family cars run on hydrogen.
♦ *Computers*: Combined computer/TV in most rooms.
♦ *Climate change*: Sea levels rise drowning a number of countries/islands.

Simulated Test Markets (STMs) were described in Chapter 6 and defined as a range of research techniques and models used to help simulate what might actually happen in a marketplace in the event of changes in certain marketing variables and/or the introduction of new products can be predicted. As such they are another form of research used to predict the future, in this case the future performance of a brand's sales or share of market

Accuracy of prediction is the desired output from this sort of research but as discussed earlier is notoriously difficult given the number of variables that need to be considered.

Scenario planning

Scenario planning is not a research technique in itself and it does not aim to predict the future, but as it extensively uses existing and trend-based research as one input and helps companies consider what they might do in the future it is worth considering in the context of this chapter.

Perhaps the most famous use of scenario planning was undertaken by Shell. Early in the 1970s, Pierre Wack and his team considered what they might do in the event of a number of different scenarios, one of which postulated that there was an unexpected event resulting in a sudden oil crisis. When the energy crisis that followed the Yom Kippur war began to unfold, Shell was better prepared and so was able to react quicker and more appropriately than its competitors. As Pierre Wack said in his famous account in the *Havard Business Review*, 'Scenarios: Shooting the Rapids', Shell's scenario planning had

> *... focused less on predicting outcomes and more on understanding the forces that would eventually compel an outcome; less on figures and more on insight.*

Scenario planning recognises that it is a mistake to assume that the future is fixed or pre-determined. Its aim is to explore some of the ways in which the future might unfold so that steps can be taken to prepare for the long-term and possible future events. It seeks to challenge what people are comfortable with. It should make people more aware of the likely lead indicators to track, which competitors to monitor and what cost/benefit assumptions to check. Michael Porter in *Competitive Advantage* defined scenarios as

> *An internally consistent view of what the future might turn out to be – not a forecast, but one possible future outcome.*

Gill Ringland in *Scenario Planning: Managing for the Future* repeats the idea that a scenario is not meant to paint a definitive picture of the future when she suggests that you should

> *Think of a scenario as a fairytale*

and scenario panning as

> *That part of strategic planning which relates to the tools and technologies for managing the uncertainties of the future.*

Scenario planning can therefore be seen as the process of generating and analysing a small set of scenarios that are relevant to a particular decision or a company's long-term performance.

The first stage of the process is normally a situational analysis whereby all relevant information and research is reviewed/compiled so the key drivers of change can be identified. This can then be assessed for impact, likelihood and what if any ability to influence the company has on them.

These drivers of change can then be used to generate alternative (often diametrically opposed) scenarios. However, the trick is not in labouring the details of the scenarios themselves, though they should be plausible, internally consistent and relevant, but rather in discussing the questions arising from and the implications of the different scenarios.

Other famous instances of effective scenario planning quoted by Gill Ringland include helping Electrolux spot new consumer markets, helping Pacific Gas and Electric prepare for the earthquake in California and helping Shell (again) anticipate the fall of Communism in Russia and its effect on natural gas prices.

Consumer involvement in innovation

Despite all that was described earlier in this chapter about the scepticism that many people have about consumer involvement in predicting the future, many companies such as Unilever, Diageo and Nestle are committed to involving them in the innovation process. As Liz Grierson, Innovation Strategist at Nestle Rowntree, says:

*We're using consumers more actively and involving them in
the right stages of the innovation process. Consumers today
are incredibly marketing literate, which has its own problems,
but it means you can talk to them in ways that you didn't
think you could.*

Traditional discussion and consumer workshops are extensively used to try to identify unmet consumer needs and how
they might be addressed. This is exploratory research (Who do
you want?) rather than evaluative research (Would you like
this?). As such, consumers are helping not only predict the
future but they are actually shaping it as smart companies
recognise that answering currently unmet needs with new
products and services is a great way to build future markets
and profits.

However, not everyone is converted. Although he did rely
on a piece of market research (or was it really PR?) when starting the company, Richard Reed, managing director at Innocent
Smoothies, says:

*I'd rather ask the 29 people at Innocent that know what we're
trying to achieve than 8 people off the street.*

The 'research' involved five-hundred bottles of juice, two bins
– one labelled YES, the other NO, a stall and a sign saying,
'Shall we give up our jobs?' The YES bin was full at the end of
the day and the new brand was launched.

One area in which research often cannot help is what has
been called the 'vision thing'. Many great brands were not
based on the purist marketing principles of identifying what
consumers want and then meeting those needs; rather they
were based on the ideals (and sometimes obsessions) of a person or group of people. Without the vision thing there would
be no Kellogg's, Disney or The Body Shop. Market research
probably would not have helped shape, guide, let alone deter
the founders of these brands who were driven by their
dreams, beliefs and ideals.

11

What is stimulus material and what does it stimulate?

Perhaps the best-known abbreviation in market research is GIGO, which stands for 'Garbage in, Garbage out'. It describes one of the biggest concerns for anyone undertaking a piece of research, namely that if the material put into the research to help gauge or stimulate a response is poor then the results coming out will be at best unreliable and at worst useless.

Stephen Wells of Wells & Co, a leading UK qualitative researcher, says, 'Quite simply, the best stimulus material should stimulate'. What he means by this statement is that the role of any materials put into research is to simulate a response. Whether that is a positive or negative response is not the issue, as it is possible to learn from either strong positive or strong negative reactions. Indeed many researchers say that they often learn more from what people do not like and why than they do from moderately positive responses. It is much harder to judge something that prompts no response or a general, ambivalent response of 'That's okay'.

Direct or indirect

More formally the roles of stimulus materials are often described as:

◆ Conveying ideas
◆ Dramatising ideas
◆ Exploring ideas
◆ Evaluating ideas.

They are generally characterised as either direct or indirect. Direct stimulus materials are those that aim to communicate an idea or concept, such as a new advertising campaign, a new packaging design or a new product. They are rough and/or outline presentations of that idea. Indirect stimulus acts to try to trigger a response from respondents to an area of inquiry, such as 'dieting' or 'sponsorship'. These also include more projective stimulus materials.

There is a huge variety of stimulus material, ranging from the very basic to the highly sophisticated.

Direct stimulus materials include:

◆ Written and/or visual concepts
◆ Product propositions
◆ Product substantiators/reasons to believe
◆ Articles/press releases
◆ Narrative tapes
◆ Talkie tapes
◆ 3D concepts (packs etc.)
◆ Product samples
◆ Mock-up print campaigns
◆ Story boards
◆ Animatics
◆ Stealomatics.

Indirect stimulus materials include:

◆ Visual prompt boards
◆ Selected imagery/tearsheets
◆ Other prompt materials (e.g. private response material)
◆ 'Touchy feely' materials.

Direct stimulus materials

Written and/or visual concepts
These are widely used to aid evaluation of product, proposition and even substantiator (reasons to believe) concepts. They can be solely verbal statements, purely visual boards to convey tone and emotional dimensions or a mix of both.

In the early stages of research, concepts tend to be short sentences that can be supported by a few images. Concepts generally become more sophisticated as they progress through development. So that a concept that started as '*An exciting new drink from the makers of Malibu'*, which was used to prompt spontaneous ideas from respondents, can be developed into a fuller concept (see below).

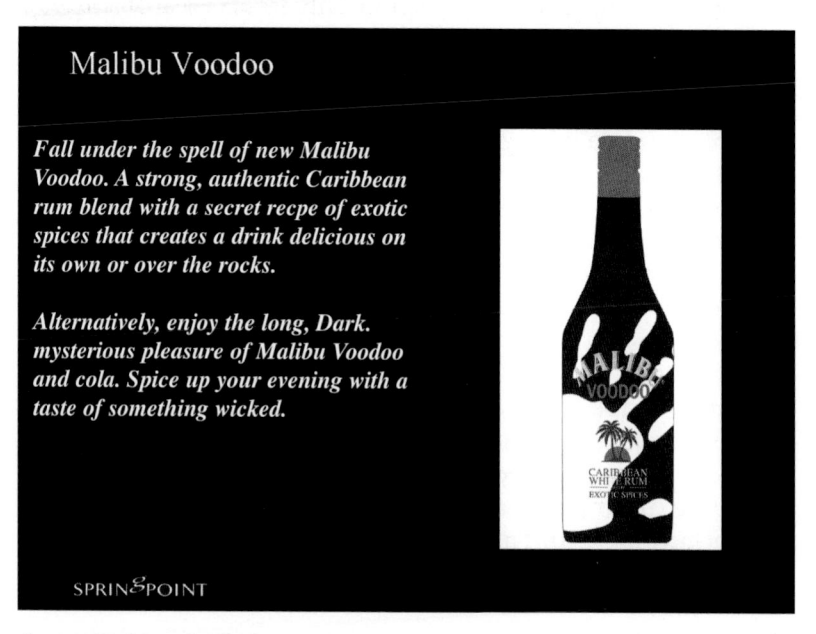

Source: Springpoint Ltd

The table below sets out the levels of information that can be included in a concept as it develops from simple to complex.

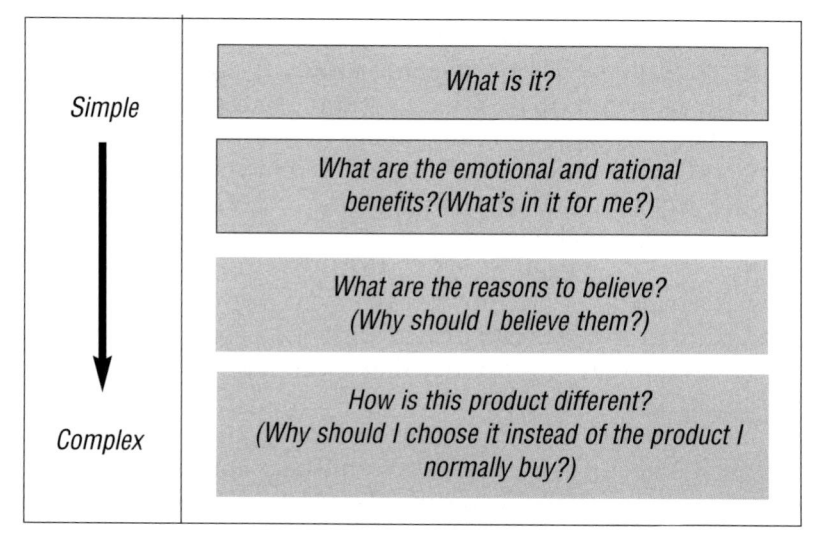

Articles/press releases
Articles/press releases are a means of bringing a concept to life in a form most consumers are familiar with. They facilitate evaluation of detailed benefit and substantiator information and can also introduce relevant tone of voice (i.e. teenage magazine versus broadsheet paper). They are often used for new products when the product idea is very new or different, as its presentation in a newspaper or magazine can lend authenticity and credibility.

When researching a new and potentially controversial 'miracle' food ingredient I stimulated an article about its launch in the USA. This allowed me to present a fully rounded case for the product and ensured a lively discussion of the issues.

Narrative tapes
A narrative tape is a recording of a description of a proposed plot and sequence of scenes to bring a brand or advertising idea to life. For respondents it is similar to hearing a play script. It is useful material, particularly because it helps introduce atmosphere and a sense of drama at a limited cost.

Talkie tapes
These provide a recording of a mock conversation between two or more consumers and as such attempt to 'gently' present a product or service idea in a realistic way (via a natural conversation) rather than 'force feed' it via a selling message.

3D concepts (packs etc.)
3D or real-life mock-ups of actual products can be useful for exploring reactions to a fairly advanced product or brand concept. They help bring a brand to life as one might find it in a store and so are good for exploring different structures, graphics and finishes, and ensuring people can react to the real shape, size and feel of a product and its packaging.

Product samples
Producing prototypes can provide fast-track feedback, as they can be tested by respondents, either in advance of fieldwork or during it. There is nothing like showing, feeling, trying and tasting what you're being asked to talk about! However, the down side is that it is easy then to mistake any prototype for the real thing and the final article. Therefore, it is important for

Source: Ziggurat

moderators to watch out for respondents getting hung up on what are actually executional details.

Mock-up print campaigns
This is material used to test print advertising campaign concepts. Most often this includes an image, the headline and strap line, but not the full body copy. If there are a number of executions they can be introduced sequentially or all together as a gallery.

Storyboards
This is comic-strip-style material often used to explore early stage TV ad concepts. It involves splitting a proposed commercial into a limited number of visuals and providing either a script for the moderator to read through as they are shown the visual or a pre-recorded tape of the script. They can help provide an approximation of the flow and feel of a commercial at a limited cost. Storyboards can also be used in new product development research to introduce how a new product works – the different stages of a product process are depicted on separate boards.

However, some people will argue that there are still some

limitations to this approach – perhaps best summed up by Bill Bernbach of the advertising agency Doyle Dane Bernbach who famously said, 'You can't storyboard a smile'.

Animatics
Animatics are an animated version of a storyboard often with

voice-over, sound effects and music. As such, they provide a basic sense of pace, mood and tone for an ad campaign. It has often been said that they are like 'Captain Pugwash' versions of commercials. They tell the story using visuals and audio but it is important to remember that they cannot convey the true feel of the final photographed film.

Stealomatics
These are video montages that are literally 'stolen' (or rather borrowed!) from existing films, ads and images and then combined with sound effects, music tracks and sometimes voice-overs. Stealomatics are often used to bring a TV ad campaign to life in a way that introduces tone, pace and mood or to demonstrate a particular filmic technique. They are also used increasingly to articulate a brand concept. The information we all consume is ever more audio-visual and so the more static mood board and written concept are less in touch with how we consume media as well as being less impactful.

Indirect stimulus materials

Visual (prompt) boards
Some visual boards work as prompt boards as part of a projective technique, for example describing a brand's personality in relation to an animal, a famous person or a car. The boards show a range of different animals, famous people or cars to help people think of analogies and comparisons.

Source: Courtesy of HPI

Selected imagery/tearsheets

Sometimes a range of imagery is supplied and used by the respondent to create their own mood board. The range of imagery may be of an idea, a concept or simply a visual depiction of their attitudes towards a particular brand.

Other prompt materials

There is a variety of prompt materials, for example bubble diagrams to capture private responses, which, while interesting in their own right, can also anchor individual reactions within a group. These materials are a projective technique used to get people to 'project' their feelings or attitudes in these instances on to an imaginary third person.

The following are examples of materials used to capture private responses:

Imagine this person just saw that ad on TV,
what would they be thinking?

Imagine this person just read that ad in a magazine or newspaper, what would they be thinking?

'Touchy feely' materials

When exploring sensory cues and dimensions, it can be useful to provoke reactions from respondents by using tactile materials. This can facilitate responses that might otherwise be difficult to elicit.

In one piece of research into a range of frozen chicken nuggets, I used Play-doh to get groups of mums to model the ideal size and shape of the nuggets they wanted for their children. After only a couple of groups it was apparent that roughly the same size products were being modelled. More importantly mums wanted to see two or three irregular shapes in every pack as they felt this would reassure them that the products were more natural. This insight was invaluable to the chefs and product development team.

12
What, if any, regulation governs market research?

Market research depends on the co-operation and participation of the general public – you and me. The industry, its clients and the agencies that conduct the research rely on people giving up their time to be interviewed and thus providing the information on what they do and do not do, what they like and do not like.

And as the future of market research depends on the continuing participation of the general public, it is not surprising that there are codes of practice and guidelines devised by the industry to set parameters for what can and cannot be done and what is and is not acceptable. Additionally, and ultimately, there are a variety of laws that help protect the rights of individuals – their right to privacy and their rights in connection with any information they choose to provide.

One of the main pieces of regulation that affects market research in the UK is therefore the Data Protection Act 1998. It does not have ten commandments; instead it has eight principles:

The Eight Data Protection Principles

The First Principle
Personal data shall be processed fairly and lawfully.

The Second Principle
Personal data shall be obtained only for one or more specified and lawful purposes, and shall not be further processed in any manner incompatible with that purpose or those purposes.

The Third Principle
Personal data shall be adequate, relevant and not excessive in relation to the purpose or purposes for which they are processed.

The Fourth Principle
Personal data shall be accurate and, where necessary, kept up to date.

The Fifth Principle
Personal data processed for any purpose or purposes shall not be kept longer than is necessary for that purpose or those purposes.

The Sixth Principle
Personal data shall be processed in accordance with the rights of data subjects under this Act.

The Seventh Principle
Appropriate technical and organisational measures shall be taken against unauthorised or unlawful processing of personal data and against accidental loss or destruction of, or damage to, personal data.

The Eighth Principle
Personal data shall not be transferred to a country or territory outside the European Economic Area, unless that country or territory ensures an adequate level of protection for the rights and freedoms of data subjects in relation to the processing of personal data.

However, probably the most used and referred source of day-to-day information about the governance of market research is the MRS Code of Conduct.

With over 8,000 members in over 50 countries, the MRS is the world's largest international membership organisation for professional researchers and others engaged or interested in market, social and opinion research. The MRS has a diverse membership comprising individual researchers within agencies, independent consultancies, client-side organisations and the academic community, as well as people from all levels of seniority and job functions. All members agree to uphold a Code of Conduct and comply with a series of specialist guidelines. Both the Code and the Guidelines are, in turn, regulated by the PSC (Professional Standards Committee). The 1999 revision of the Code says:

The Code of Conduct is designed to support all those engaged in marketing or social research in maintaining professional standards. It applies to all members of The Market Research

Society, whether they are engaged in consumer, business-to-business, social, opinion or any other type of confidential survey research. It applies to all quantitative and qualitative methods for data gathering. Assurance that research is conducted in an ethical manner is needed to create confidence in, and to encourage co-operation among the business community, the general public, regulators and others.

The Code of Conduct does not take precedence over national law. Members responsible for international research shall take its provisions as a minimum requirement and fulfil any other responsibilities set down in law or by nationally agreed standards.

The MRS Guidelines exist or are being developed in many new areas in order to provide a comprehensive framework of interpretation. They have been (or are being) written to take account of the increasingly diverse activities of the Society's members, some of which are not covered in detail by the Code of Conduct.

A full list of guidelines is available on the Society's website or from the Society's Standards Manager, but they include specific material for

◆ Qualitative research
◆ Quantitative data collection
◆ Questionnaire design
◆ Research among children and young people
◆ Employee research
◆ The responsibilities of interviewers.

There are also a number of legal guidelines to help market researchers adhere to the Data Protection Act and a number of draft guidelines on such subjects as Internet research, observational research, public opinion research and business-to-business research.

Like the Data Protection Act, the Code is based on a set of principles. The most fundamental of these principles are: Firstly, nobody involved in any research should be misled as to what they are involved in. If they are told that they are involved in some market research they need to be reassured that they will not be 'sold to' during the session or pestered

with any follow-up sales calls. In other words, the only purpose of research should be:

> *... to collect and analyse information, and not directly to cre-*
> *ate sales nor to influence the opinions of anyone participating*
> *in it.*

> *Wherever possible respondents must be informed as to the pur-*
> *pose of the research and the likely length of time necessary for*
> *the collection of the information.*

Secondly, if people are told that the research is confidential
then this must be respected. Their views can be expressed and
attributed anonymously but their names and details must not
be released to anyone without their specific permission:

> *They must be assured that no information which could be used*
> *to identify them will be made available without their agree-*
> *ment to anyone outside the agency responsible for conducting*
> *the research.*

Finally, and perhaps the hardest to assess, particularly in qualitative research, the Code demands that

> *the research findings themselves must always be reported*
> *accurately and never used to mislead anyone, in any way.*

So, in short, the overriding principle of the MRS Code of
Conduct can be summarised thus: that research should always
be

> *conducted honestly, objectively, without unwelcome intru-*
> *sion and without harm to respondents.*

It is perhaps interesting to compare this with advertising's
Code of Practice, the overriding aim of which is to ensure
every ad is 'legal, decent, honest and truthful'. Experience,
however, suggests that the market research industry, though
not perfect, lives up to its Code much better than the advertising industry, where agencies seem to want to continually push
their code to its limits.

13

Do research and creativity mix?

One of the main uses of market research today is to aid in the creation and development of advertising campaigns. Despite its extensive application, the debate as to whether or not research and creativity are really compatible still rumbles, even if it no longer rages.

On one hand, clients wish to avoid the 'hit and miss' nature of creative development; on the other hand, some agencies, or agency 'creatives', still, at least privately, believe research kills off many great ideas before they are fully formed. They argue that research is unable to deal with radically new concepts and is too heavy handed when they play back the 'superficial' responses of consumers who do not know how to react.

One apocryphal story told in P.R. Smith's *Marketing Communications: An Integrated Approach,* as well as by numerous creative directors, is that of the Heineken's 'Refreshes the parts …' campaign.

One of [the] UK's most successful advertising campaigns 'Heineken refreshes the parts other beers cannot reach' had the normal focus groups/concept research carried out. It 'researched poorly', i.e. the results said, 'This is rubbish. We don't understand this type of ad. Don't do it.'

Frank Lowe (chairman of the advertising agency Lowe Howard Spink) tells the story of how he had to tell his client about the negative concept research findings on their radically different advertising concept.

'He (the client) took a very brave decision and placed the research report document in the bin. He said, "We'd best leave that alone and get on with the ad!"'

Expensive and carefully prepared research findings are sometimes ignored.

Whilst in this case this proved to be the right choice – the campaign went on to be one of the most successful alcoholic drinks' campaigns of all time – there are instances where the research results suggested that a creative idea should not be progressed and when the results were ignored, an unsuccessful campaign was developed. Large sums of money were then wasted. There are also numerous positive examples of different types of research aiding in the creation, development and refinement of creative ideas.

Research your product until it squeaks

David Ogilvy always said that you should 'interrogate a product until it squeaks' and that this product research (not really market research) led him to be able to create such famous ads as:

> *'The loudest sound in this Rolls Royce travelling at 60m.p.h. is the ticking of the clock.'*

There are numerous examples of 'market research' facts being used in advertising, they include:

> *In research 9 out of 10 owners, who expressed a preference, said their cats preferred Whiskas.*

> *Every 15 minutes someone is being reconnected to BT.*

The different stages of creative development

Sue Gardiner and I wrote a paper that was lucky enough to win a gold prize at The AMSO Research Effectiveness in 1993. It demonstrated how research played a crucial role in developing and refining the launch ad for Oxo Gravy Granules. One of the stated aims was

> *... to demonstrate that quantified research and creativity can and do mix – and that well done can be of fundamental value in developing highly effective advertising.*

The paper showed how tracking studies helped highlight that the Family campaign, featuring Lynda Bellingham, was, despite its effectiveness, fighting a losing battle. People's product usage was shifting away from cubes to granules and even a highly successful advertising campaign could not make up for a lack of new product development.

Perhaps most importantly the tracking studies also showed that in previous commercials featuring the launch of a new Oxo product there was a danger that the recall from the commercial would 'default' to Red (Beef) Oxo, the dominant product in the range, unless care was taken in structuring the commercial. The new product needed to be intrinsically woven into the main plot of any family commercial. This learning was incorporated in the creative brief.

Finally, the paper showed how the ad was pre-tested and that the results were used to further ensure the key theme of mistaking gravy for coffee granules was maintained right through to the end of the commercial, ensuring optimum recall of the new product and not just Red (Beef) Oxo.

The final ad went on to become one of the most successful ads in the long-running series of ads. In fact, the ad was so successful that it had to be withdrawn for a period because the factory could not keep up with the demand!

We started our paper with the dilemma which faced Oxo – it had an extraordinarily strong campaign that had gone as far as it could to sustain Oxo market share without a strategic product launch. We have followed the development of that launch and the use of the strength of the existing Oxo campaign. Most importantly we have looked at the value of tracking and pre-testing research techniques to that launch in:

◆ *Identifying the opportunities*
◆ *Refining the communication of the launch idea within the campaign*
◆ *Understanding the relevance of the new product to the image of the brand as a whole.*

Clearly the most resounding postscript to our marketing research endeavours is the fact that the launch worked. We'll leave you with the sales data.

Sterling Share Total Gravy Market	1984 (Pre-Oxo NPD)	1988 (Post-Granules Launch)	January 1992
Oxo	26	24	33
Bisto	30	33	34
Others	44	43	33

The creativity versus research debate tends to focus on the evaluation and optimisation of early creative ideas but this is in fact only one stage of research for advertising development. It is worth considering the full process to review the different roles that research plays and to understand that research can influence creativity in a number of ways. In *Managing Advertising*, Gavin Galloway sets out the full process:

Research (and information) for advertising development covers a lengthy sequence of procedures that progress from broad/general to highly focused/specific.

It is essential to start at the beginning and work through systematically: if this is not done, the resulting advertising (and other communications) will be built on shaky foundations.

Step 1   Review your brand in its consumer market and broader economic context; use this appraisal to set realistic goals for the brand and its communication programme.

Step 2   Use early development research (before agreeing the creative brief) to better understand the current consumer context and, if necessary, to re-appraise the brand positioning.

Step 3   Use creative development research to help evaluate and optimise early creative ideas.

Step 4   Use pre-test research to evaluate the likely effect of your finished advertising on consumer behaviour and perceptions of the brand.

The Oxo Gravy Granule ad example quoted earlier shows how 'Step 4', a pre-test, helped identify a potential weakness of a proposed script and goes on to suggest a way in which the issue might be solved.

Another example of research at a different stage aiding in the creation of an idea is that of the AA's 'Fourth Emergency Service' campaign. The whole concept for this advertising campaign arose out of some early development research, Step 2. This research, conducted by AA's then advertising agency HHCL + Partners, looked at, among other things, how AA men were viewed and treated by its customers. The research identified that the most frequent contact people had with AA personnel was if and when their car broke down. This meant that they were delighted to see the AA personnel coming to rescue them from an 'emergency' and that they treated them in much the same way as the police, firemen and ambulance services. This insight from a piece of research can clearly be seen as the inspiration for the campaign.

In the early 1990s, research undertaken by HPI demonstrated that people had become increasingly blasé about the threat of losing their licence if caught drink driving. However, what the research simultaneously identified was that drink driving was being seen as more and more socially irresponsible. Based on this insight, there was a shift in creative strategy and a new and highly successful government-funded ad campaign was developed.

Indeed, the whole Oxo Family campaign idea (of which the Gravy Granule ad discussed earlier was one execution) also came out of early development research into family life. The research provided the insights for the basic campaign idea and the specifics for many of the different commercials themselves. The original piece of research was unusual in so far as it did not centre on the brand or even the stock cube market, rather it explored family life and how it was portrayed on TV at that time (early 1980s).

It identified two insights: firstly, that modern family life was a mixture of grief and relief, trails and tribulations, difficulties and disasters offset by the odd highly valued moment of pleasure; and secondly, that back in 1980, other media was pulling ahead of its presentation of families. Programmes such as *Butterflies*, in which Wendy Craig tried to cope with a dour

Photo: John Claridge

WE'RE BIG ENOUGH TO SAY WE'RE Nº4

TO OUR MEMBERS WE'RE THE 4TH EMERGENCY SERVICE

AA

The Fourth Emercency Service

From being those very nice men who helped when your car broke down the AA has re-positioned itself as 'The Fourth Emercency Service'.

husband and two teenage boys, and the soap opera *Brookside* were starting to reflect the realities of everyday life much more honestly than commercials. Advertising of that time was full of perfect families with attractive mums, handsome dads and cherubic children who behaved beautifully. Somebody in one group summed it up perfectly as

Plastic people with plastic smiles.

Most of the people researched had had enough of it and longed for a more adult, realistic and empathetic portrayal of families in advertising. So what the research had effectively revealed was that there was an opportunity for a brand to reflect real family life more accurately. The research had provided insights into what it was really like – all that was left for the creative team was to use this guidance, which they did to great effect.

Nowadays most people in the marketing and agency world accept that research does have a role to play in helping develop and evaluate creative ideas, whether they are advertising campaigns, new corporate identities or packaging design.

14

Why is there such interest in insight?

We're all using the same techniques to ask the same consumers the same questions; it's not surprising therefore that we're all getting to the same answers.

This is an oft-quoted adage, which undoubtedly has more than a drop of truth in it. Nearly every major company in the world conducts significant amounts of market research every year. For much of this research they use exactly the same or at least the same sort of market research agency. These agencies use broadly similar techniques (though they may call them different names) and they usually talk to the same sort of people.

Take for example the detergents market. Whether you are Persil or Ariel you will still talk predominantly to those who do the purchasing of washing powders and those who use them in the home. You will want to look at your heavy users and probably your main competitors' heavy users. You will probably want to research your non-users – the users of your competition. As Persil and Ariel are the main two brands they will be looking at their own and each other's users.

Whether you are Persil or Ariel you will want to know the same sort of information:

◆ What do they want from a washing powder?
◆ What do they do well?
◆ What don't they do well?
◆ What could/should be improved?
◆ What sorts of clothes are they washing?
◆ What are they washing more of and what are they washing less of?
◆ How do they do their washing? (Identifying the whites, lights and colours separate washes led Ariel to launch Ariel Colour)
◆ Why do they choose the brand they do?

◆ What do they think/feel about their brand and the competition?
◆ What might make them swap brands?
◆ Do they think they get value for money?
◆ Do they remember my/my competitors' advertising?
◆ What does it tell them?
◆ What does it make them feel about my brand?

Given this consistency of approach and the subsequent similarity of answers it is not surprising that market research departments in these companies are looking for increased speed and responsiveness in research, new innovative research techniques and more probing questions.

Additionally, over the last twenty years there has been an exponential growth in the amount of both hard and soft data available to market researchers and marketers. In most companies more and more research is being undertaken and more reports are being published and made publicly available by the government, NGOs, think tanks, the media and pressure groups.

Developments such as the loyalty card mean that data is now not just available on panels of 10–20,000 people, but that specific actual purchasing information, regularly updated, is available on samples of 5–10 million people. Market researchers are in danger of drowning in a sea of data.

Insight

The combination of data overload and a consistency over best practice has also led to researchers and market research companies placing increasing emphasis on 'insight'. Indeed, 'insight' has become the 'holy grail' of the market research industry. Market research departments are looking for it and market research companies are claiming that they can help you find it.

Insight has been defined as a penetrating understanding that drives profitable growth. Paul Walton of the Value Engineers calls insights

The triple word scores of research …

… reflecting the fact that they are often derived from the same ingredients/sources as other research but can be much more valuable.

A broad definition of insight is that it is the 'process' by which market or consumer data is rapidly translated into actionable knowledge through a specific finding or interpretation that is particularly incisive. The net result of this is that the company or brand can use the information to develop an idea or concept before its competitors, so creating extra sales and/or profit.

Insights therefore have one or more of the following characteristics:

◆ At their heart there is a piece of understanding that is particularly illuminating. It goes beyond the accepted norms or truisms of the market. Some insights once identified can evoke a 'Why didn't we think of that earlier?' response.

◆ They can be translated in action for a particular brand or company. The true value of insights, like all market research, is not measured by the inherent quality or even the originality of the thinking but by the ability of those receiving the information to do something constructive with it.

◆ They are arrived at quickly and, ideally, before your competitors. Insight has been likened to the ability to spot a 'pattern' and so insights are often referred to as 'Aa-ah! moments' when suddenly something/everything falls into place. The real benefit of these moments comes when you have your 'Aa-ah! moment' before your competitor, giving you a competitive advantage.

◆ They deliver a financial benefit to the brand or company. The ultimate benefit of insight is to generate additional sales, new products or services, cost reductions and so increased profits.

If, as I have suggested, most researchers are currently using broadly the same techniques, then the drive to uncover insights suggests two alternative strategies for research companies and market research departments. Either they should place an increased emphasis on perceptive and informative analysis and interpretation or they should look for new approaches.

Perhaps predictably, what seems to be happening is the latter. There has, in recent years, been a great deal of pressure for, and increasing experimentation with, alternative methodologies. People are continually looking for the next big thing in research. There was a flurry of interest in semiotics in the mid-1990s and more recently considerable interest in ethnographic and anthropological approaches. Most recently, there seems to be a growing interest in 'memes'. In his book *After Image*, John Grant describes the origin of 'memes':

> *The word 'meme' first surfaced in 1976 in a book called* The Selfish Gene *by Richard Dawkins. He wanted to illustrate his idea of 'evolution as replication'. So he came up with an example: the 'mimeme' (shortened to 'meme' to sound like 'gene') which is a 'unit of cultural transmission' or 'unit of imitation'.*

Grant goes on to note that whilst Dawkins' main examples are religious and scientific ideas he also talks about the potential for 'tunes, ideas, catchphrases, clothes, fashions' to be memes.

The theory of memes concerns how an idea takes root and then spreads rapidly, like a virus, and so the theory of memes is itself a perfect example of a powerful meme. Marketing people – and therefore market research – are not surprisingly interested in any theories about how to spread a new idea rapidly. So you can expect to hear more about them and research techniques for identifying and improving them.

The search for insight will continue, however, as it is a central issue for the future of market research. Some of the merging formal and informal techniques and some predictions on the future for market research are covered in later chapters. However, before leaving the topic of insight it is worth noting one final side effect of this overwhelming desire for insights: increasingly, you cannot find market research managers in companies anymore; what you will find are hundreds and hundreds of 'consumer insight managers'.

Every company seems to have identified this need for more telling research and they have all decided to re-brand themselves, proving yet again that everyone is getting to the same answers at about the same time (or that the notion of insight being more important and valuable than 'mere market research' is a powerful meme!).

15

What is informal research?

In his book *Company Man: The Rise and Fall of Corporate Life*, Anthony Sampson tells the story of how Virgin Atlantic was born not on the basis of reams and reams of formal market research but a much smaller and more informal piece of research conducted by Sir Richard Branson himself.

When he started his Virgin airline in 1984 it seemed a rash and surprising switch: 'I decided there must be room for another airline when I spent two days trying to get through to People Express,' he (Sir Richard Branson) told me on his barge. 'That was the sum of my market research'.

This predilection for informal research still remains at Virgin. Will Whitehorn, the Corporate Affairs Director, always says that some of his best research is also the cheapest. He buys the *Sun* newspaper everyday. His view is that it helps him keep his finger on the pulse of public opinion and trends by reading it. It costs him (currently) all of 30p a day.

Chris Forrest and Terry Prue in their chapter 'Advertising Research' tell how new more informal techniques are developed to address specific situations. They describe how some years ago, when faced with a decline in image and sales, Polaroid invented a new photography-led market research technique. Employees of their advertising agency, BBH, were given a Polaroid camera and a conventional camera for a week and then asked to use them when they thought it seemed appropriate. This 'social experiment' showed them that people were often embarrassed to be seen using a Polaroid. It was perceived as a bit 'naff' and 'uncool'.

However, when the photos were reviewed interesting and insightful differences were seen. People tended to 'compose' themselves formally for the conventional camera but they were much more relaxed in the Polaroid photos. They felt free to act up, pull faces and have fun for the Polaroid precisely because they did not take it too seriously. What this suggested was that there was a flip side to any 'naffness' – a Polaroid camera could have a role as a 'lubricant of social interaction' or, more colloquially, could help to get things going. This proved to be valuable learning in the development of the brand positioning, new products and in particular in this case new advertising. As Forrest and Prue conclude:

> *[Advertising] agencies are often desperately searching for an 'angle', an insight that can get them to a more powerful proposition. Since necessity is the mother of invention, they can be pretty inventive.*

Thus it can be seen that relevant and useful learning does not always come from formal research.

Now, if formal research is defined (by Philip Kotler) as

> *The systematic design, collection, analysis and reporting of data relevant to a specific marketing situation facing the company*

then informal research could be defined as

> *The random observation, contemplation, intuition and sharing of little snippets of information which may or may not at first seem directly relevant to any marketing situation.*

Therefore, informal research is not usually conducted by research agencies but is based on personal observation, very small samples or by what Faith Popcorn, the doyenne of *American Futurology*, calls 'brailing the culture'. This includes everything from talking to cab drivers, to reading a different magazine or newspaper every week and to observing what is going on around you.

For example, picking up my sons from school the other day I was people watching, as usual, and happened to note what the other parents were wearing. It is a school of around 600 pupils; most children are picked up by one of their parents, usually their mothers. What struck me was that out of at least 200 women, only 6 were wearing skirts. It was early spring, neither particularly cold nor hot and it was not raining. Now, I understand that you do not dress up to collect children from school but I was struck by the shift away from skirts and towards trousers. No wonder, I thought, so many hosiery companies are trying to extend their brands into new markets.

Later that same day I was in a restaurant with some clients and as ever I was taking an age to read the menu. While on occasion I may be slow to choose what I am actually going to eat, I always take ages over the menu. That is because I study or rather 'research' menus.

Menus are a great source of informal research if you work on any food brand. It pays to look at how the dishes are described. What are the 'hot' ingredients? What are the new dishes? Comparing and contrasting different menus, especially the differences between everyday and more sophisticated ones, can be an interesting source of information. When did Thai or the latest hot country cuisine make it onto everyday restaurant menus like Harvester's? How long did it take for 'roasted vegetables' to move from the Ivy restaurant to Iceland stores?

Whilst formal 'garbology' and trained 'garbologists' do exist – Dr William Rathje, head of the Garbage Project at Arizona University, is said to be the world's leading expert with over thirty years spent studying people's garbage – a more informal approach to 'rubbishwatching' can help you recognise emerging tastes and trends. What are the most prevalent brands of soft drink cans and/or sweets, crisps or savoury snack wrappers you see lying in the street? My casual observations told me when Tango was really on the up and I spotted the almost overnight impact of Sunny Delight in the UK, not in the marketing press, but from the streets around my hometown and especially around the schools.

(By the way, in case you're interested, the worst smelling garbage according to Dr Rathje is raw, spoilt chicken: 'It's bad enough to make anyone turn and run,' he says.)

Another form of 'informal research' that is increasingly being implemented by a number of large companies (and thereby becoming more 'formal') is regular consumer contact, sometimes known as consumer connection. Here everybody in the marketing and sometimes the product development department is encouraged to go out and conduct their own interviews with 'consumers'.

Meeting your customer has been taken a lot further by a number of agencies that now organise 'field trips' for marketing departments so they can watch and learn from their consumers in their natural 'habitats'. So, for example, Vegas, a division of trbi (The Research Business International) that specialises in research and brand development for contemporary and youth-targeted brands, has organised trips to clubs and music festivals for a number of clients.

Whilst this is unlikely ever to replace more formal research it does help these people keep in touch with their customers and their lives. It does not aim to address specific marketing issues like a new advertising or packaging approach but rather it can help provide the interviewers (the marketers) with a more realistic understanding of their customers and their lives. It is particularly useful when you consider that in some cases a brand manager might be a young twenty-something single man and he might be looking after a brand targeted at mothers with young children.

In fact, a basic understanding of family life might have stopped one brand I know launching a promotion that consisted of six fish fingers, two potato waffles and peas for two but included only *one* free toy. It proved to be a recipe not for a happy meal, but for sibling squabbling, as any parent would have told them immediately.

I worked with a very large media company where the research department was very concerned that the senior management was taking the level of complaints and dissatisfaction with their brand very complacently. The level of dissatisfaction as measured in their regular tracking studies was reasonably high but because the figures were also relatively static, they were being ignored.

We arranged a series of customer and importantly ex-customer workshops, which a number of the board attended. It was a real eye opener for them and helped them get a much better insight in some of the issues and frustrations of their customers. Their dissatisfied customers stopped being just another number when they were in direct discussion with them. One of the other advantages of this sort of research with the most senior management in the company was that this was also one of the instances where suggested changes were implemented very, very quickly!

Informal research is not the answer to all management questions and there is a serious health warning that needs to be considered. Informal research is, as the name suggests informal; it does not have the discipline, structure or rigour that is inherent within formal research. Sample sizes are small (they can be one person), the samples can be very biased (your family, friends and your hometown may not be very representative) and the person doing the interpretation (you) may not have been trained or be very experienced at it.

It is important to remember that for every story like the foundation of Virgin Atlantic, there are stories like that of Sir Clive Sinclair's C5 where undertaking no formal research can be an expensive error of judgement. Sir Clive Sinclair had revolutionised the computer industry in the UK when he introduced the Spectrum ZX computer onto the market. Its combination of high power and low price set it apart from its competitors and helped broaden the market for home computers. The ZX led the field in computers and needed little market research.

Sir Clive's dream was to produce an easily affordable and practical electric car – the C5. He announced that he intended to change the way we drove and that 'the petrol engine would be a thing of the past' by the end of the 20th century. Having had enormous success without relying on market research and now developing another cutting-edge, potentially life- and society-changing product (which market research might find hard to evaluate), Sinclair is said to have conducted little or no market research.

The means to achieve this fundamental shift in society was unveiled at Alexander Palace on 10 January 1985. It was an open-topped, single-seat, lightweight, three-wheeled electric car, which was to become known as the C5. It measured 31 inches off the ground and had no steering wheel but was manoeuvred by a handlebar underneath the drivers' thighs. Sinclair claimed that powered by its washing-machine motor it had a top speed of 14 miles an hour and a range of about 20 miles before it needed recharging.

Despite enormous media interest and a PR frenzy the C5 bombed. Whilst Sir Clive admitted that he thought it would be 'a cultural shock for the motorist' he said he hoped to sell 100,000 C5s in their first year at £399 each. However, despite launching special conversion kits, PR initiatives and huge price cuts, Sinclair Vehicles was put into receivership in October 1985. Only 4,500 C5s had been sold. It has been estimated that the venture cost Sir Clive £8.6 million of his own money. A fraction of this would have bought him some well-conducted formal market research, which would have undoubtedly told him not to go ahead.

Informal research is a useful tool in any marketer's armoury but, like its more formal brother, it has its strengths and its weaknesses.

16
What does the future hold for market research?

Having written earlier in this book about the difficulty of predicting the future, I, not surprisingly, approach this chapter with some trepidation. But as I have also said the benefits of thinking about the future don't necessarily come from getting it right, but in thinking about the assumptions and implications of any possible changes. So here are a few thoughts ...

It will continue to be a growing market

Market research in many ways cannot lose. In good times budgets exist for ongoing research as well as to try to explore new options. When things are not so good, then there is a need for research to find out what is going wrong, to help ensure money is not going to be wasted and/or to search for new alternatives.

It seems likely then that with

- ◆ the increased pressure that comes from continually delivering ever better results in the short term
- ◆ the desire, or need, to try to really get under the skin of the situation, your company or your brand so you can build a successful long-term future
- ◆ and the continuing, if not growing, need for innovation

there will need to be more, not less, market research in the future. Market research is now so intrinsically woven into most companies' approach to business that it is hard to see any reason for a decline.

Internet-based research will continue to grow

As has already been discussed, Internet-based research has exploded in popularity and usage in the USA and while Europe is some way behind, its usage is still growing rapidly here too. Internet research is fast and relatively cheap and with the spread of broadband and other technologies it can do more and more. It allows visual and increasingly audio-visual stimulus material to be shown during the course of an interview, something that cannot be done in more traditional telephone-based surveys.

Its application in qualitative research is more limited, given the preference for focus groups, but on-line groups in chat rooms are being used. The web camera also offers the opportunity for more true connectivity and interaction on-line, as well as the potential for more observational-/ethnographic-based research to be conducted on-line.

The amount of information will continue to grow

The market research market is likely to continue growing and the number of reports and amount of information published by the government, NGOs, the media, think tanks, special interest and pressure groups will also increase. The result of this will be that market researchers and marketers will face not just a flood but a veritable tsunami of data. The danger will be that they drown in data.

As mentioned earlier, one telling comparison might be between a traditional retail panel, which might include 10–20,000 respondents, versus the information available to Tesco via their Clubcard, which has somewhere in the region of 10,000,000 users! Tesco's problem is not that they do not know what is happening with their customers but that they have too much information.

The search for new techniques will continue

Existing market research users and practitioners will continue to look for and explore new techniques in the drive to keep up with the evolving marketplace and in the need to deliver better or deeper insights. This will be driven by a combination of factors:

◆ The changing marketplace with the shift towards tailored, one-to-one marketing solutions will mean that a number of the existing forecasting techniques will become less appropriate and new techniques will be required. (This was discussed in Chapter 6 in relation to STMs.)

◆ Boredom and the desire for something new will be another factor. Some users/practitioners will just feel that they have used the same old techniques for so long that they need a change.

◆ The fact that everybody is using the same techniques on the same (type of) people and getting the same answers, often at about the same time, is perhaps a more rational argument that will encourage the same sort of continuing experimentation.

This was probably the reason why a few years ago there was an upsurge in semiotic research and why currently there is huge interest in ethnographical approaches (see Chapter 15) and other more direct contact techniques like consumer workshops.

In the next few years, it may well be that the market research world borrows from other fields of academia.

Look out for 'memes' and new market research techniques to assess what will make/whether yours is an effective technique.

◆ Market research companies, as profit-making businesses, will continue to look for new business-building opportunities. They will believe that if they can find something new and different it will give them a competitive advantage.

An increased focus on integrated communication campaigns

Much of existing research has been focused on the different specific marketing communication disciplines – packaging, corporate design, promotions and most prominently advertising. However, the world of marketing communications is changing – the supremacy of advertising is being challenged.

The proportion of promotional budgets spent 'above the line' is decreasing. With ever-more fragmenting audiences, media options proliferating and still high levels of media cost inflation, brands that in the past used heavy-weight advertising as their main means of communicating with their consumers are now being forced to find different approaches.

There is also an increasing recognition of the need to understand a brand's total communication and whether or not the individual elements combine to create an integrated and hopefully synergistic whole.

The analogy is the need to assess whether or not the separate instruments of a brand's communication are creating an appealing harmony or whether they are they causing a jarring, even confusing, cacophony of mixed messages.

One company promoting this approach is HPI and in *Marketing Superglue: How to Make Brand Values Stick*, David Iddiols, one of the company's founders, discusses the three different approaches to making this work that they have identified:

Values as glue
Proposition as glue
Mnemonic as glue

He goes on to describe them:

Mnemonic as glue: Employing a mnemonic is readily recognised by consumers as a potential 'kebab skewer' running through different aspects of a marketing campaign. However, it does appear to be more powerful and apposite when a brand is entering a market ... Direct Line were able to establish an identity and gain a place in the public's consciousness through consistent and prominent use of the red phone.

Proposition as glue: Consistently imparting a proposition also makes sense when the focus is on establishing or shifting a brand's identity. Although less commonplace than the other two 'glues', participants in our research were nevertheless able to cite examples without too much difficulty, for example Tesco – Every little helps.

Values as glue: Conveying a consistent set of values is undoubtedly the strongest of the three models. Indeed it can be argued that the proposition and mnemonic-led routes are essentially the stepping-stones to creating a cohesive brand identity ... Volvo has successfully rid itself of its 'safe but boring' tag through meticulous adherence to a new set of values which promote style and performance alongside safety. This can be observed across a wide range of marketing communications.

Whilst these examples represent a good start, further development and understanding of how multi-media campaigns work and, in particular, how companies and brands can most efficiently use different media to convey different messages to two or more different key target groups and yet still create a consistent and powerful brand image are required. A classic example would be a kids' food brand, which is likely to want to appear to be cool and desirable to the kids and yet reassure their parents of the products' intrinsic 'goodness'.

The roles of the different parts of the brand's communication and their individual contribution to the overall perceptions of the brand still needs more work. Whereas in the past much research development was led by the advertising agencies and the research companies, it may well be that the communication planning/media agencies and the research agencies will come together and lead the creation of the new tools and methodologies, which can be applied across the output of a number of different creative agencies (advertising, promotions, design, brand experience, direct mail, e-marketing, PR).

Viewed focus groups will form the basis of a new TV series

Despite the search for new techniques, focus groups will continue to be used extensively. It is also highly likely that they will continue to be used by political parties and so retain a high profile amongst not just the marketing fraternity, but the general public too.

With TV's continuing search for new fly-on-the-wall series featuring real people, I would predict (suggest) that viewed focus groups on contentious subjects could be the next surprise hit of the schedules. Getting two groups with opposing views to discuss the same topic or indeed one lively conflict group could make compelling viewing if appropriately recruited and provocatively moderated.

Appendix 1
What are the questions you
should ask of any market research?

Over the years I have built up a bank of questions and a mental checklist, which provide me with a start-point when considering any piece of market research. I reproduce them here not because I think they represent the definitive list but in the hope that they may be useful to you and help you avoid many of the mistakes I made. If nothing else they should allow you to 'bluff' your way through any research debrief. It will at least seem that you know enough to be asking the right sorts of questions.

The Ten 'Commandments'

1. Focus on the strategic issues

2. Use research to discover what is not known and to provide guidance where there is uncertainty

3. View your research budget as a strategic investment – resist temptations to cut it

4. Before beginning any piece of research, specify 'action standards' to define how actions will be affected by results

5. Define the problem (and ensure you look for the problem behind the problem)

6. Regularly research your markets and products especially in major markets

7. Summarise all research thoroughly and make results understandable and comparable with past work and/or across countries

8. Make decisions based on relevant data, objectively analysed and used with judgement

9. Do not be strait-jacketed by formal research methodologies (use informal research as well)

10. Remember, first and foremost the consumer is a person – not just a sale!

Ten questions to ask about any piece of quantitative research

1. What were the specific objectives of this piece of research?

2. What exactly was being measured – actual or claimed behaviour?

3. What was the sample size?

4. What was the sample structure?

5. What were the sample sizes for any important sub-groups you might wish to analyse?

6. What were the questions?

7. When and where was the research conducted?

8. What if any are the relevant norms?

9. How good (reliable/robust) are those norms?

10. Are any of the differences statistically significant?

Ten questions to ask about any piece of qualitative research

1. What were the specific objectives of this piece of research?

2. Who conducted the research?

3. How was it conducted?

4. When and where was it conducted?

5. Amongst whom was it conducted ?

6. How does this correspond with existing and/or target users?

7. What stimulus materials were used?

8. Are the results consistent with common sense?

9. Are the results consistent with other findings?

10. Is there any quantified research to support/confirm these findings?

Appendix 2
Some basic guidelines for observers of focus groups

Before the group

◆ *Review the purpose of the research.*
What are the key reasons qualitative research is being conducted? Get a copy and read the research proposal. Compare this with your 'personal agenda'.

◆ *Review the moderator's guide and become familiar with the proposed flow of the focus group.*
Be clear on the key issues to be covered and the tasks that group respondents will be doing.

Arriving at the focus group

◆ *Arrive early, ideally 30 to 45 minutes before the scheduled start of the session.*
Your early arrival cuts down on the chance of running into participants and heightening their anxiety about who the observers are. For example, if the participants are blue-collar workers and they see a stream of people coming through the reception room dressed in suits and ties carrying leather briefcases and then later, during the introductions, are told they are being observed, they may have the experience of being 'monkeys in the zoo' because they are so different from the observers.

◆ *Try to maintain anonymity.*
Introduce yourself in such a way as to maintain corporate anonymity in case the recruiting is 'blind'. For example you could say:

'Hello. My name is ... and I'm here as part of the moderator's team. Is she/he here yet?'

Try to avoid saying anything like:

'Hello. I'm here to watch the focus group.'
'Hello. I'm from the ad agency.'
'Hello. I'm the client for the focus group study.'

Naomi Henderson, founder and CEO of RIVA (Research in Values and Attitudes), recounts a story of an inappropriate introduction that occurred during a study for a radio station in New York City:

The purpose of the research was to assess the image of that station among light and heavy listeners. The recruiting had been 'blind,' respondents didn't know which radio station was paying for the project. An early topic intended for each group was: 'What's your impression of W? What do you think of the station?' These questions were to be asked about three stations in the New York City area. It was critical to see what descriptive words were used about each station.

The focus group facility was small, and there was only one door to the suite so that clients and respondents alike had to come through the same door. At 5:45, fifteen minutes before the group was due to begin, two observers from the radio station came into the suite, briefcases in hand, and marched up to the reception desk. One of them said, in a voice loud enough for everyone to hear: 'I'm with the station manager for W, and I'm here to watch the groups.' The cat was out of the bag ... every respondent now knew which radio station was paying for the research, and any opportunity to get unbiased answers about the image of the station was lost.

This sorely compromised the research opportunity, and the advertising agency and the moderator agreed that the disclosure would adversely affect the research. Therefore, the group of (light) respondents [was] paid and sent home. That 'gaffe' cost the radio station all the costs for that group and a lost opportunity.

During the focus groups

◆ *Recognise the need for moderator flexibility.*

The moderator will not ask every question in the guide or ask the questions in the same language or order as the written guide. The qualitative process is not as rigid as a survey; good moderators will 'go with the flow' in a discussion if a rich vein of information can be unearthed. Moderators also skip questions if respondents have already covered an area or if time constraints exist.

◆ *Allow for group flexibility.*
  Do not expect:

  — Every minute of every group to be meaningful
  — Every question to have an immediate payoff in providing insight
  — Every comment, statement, response or interchange to directly relate to the topic being discussed
  — Each group in a series to provide equal data.

◆ Some questions, and the subsequent answers from respondents, are 'set-ups' or 'bridges' to move from one topic to another or to close down an area. Some questions work great on paper and not in real life. Sometimes respondents have to formulate an opinion and they do that out loud rather than internally. The process of forming that opinion may sound like rambling. Sometimes the moderator is 'backtracking' or 'future pacing' and the questions and their answers, on the surface, do not appear to be going anywhere. Expect each group to contribute to a whole understanding of the key issues, not necessarily to stand alone and provide 'the answer'.

◆ *Expect respondents to forget the ground rules from time to time.*
  Despite what they are told to do respondents are quite likely to:

  — Talk all at once
  — Talk too softly at times
  — Stray from the topic of conversation
  — Have side conversations
  — Fail to have the courage of their convictions.

◆ The group process is dynamic – the respondents feed and

stimulate each other. In the excitement of a new idea, it is natural to blurt out and all talk at once. Fear and shyness about revealing one's thoughts or beliefs can make someone talk softly or want to share only with someone nearby and not to the group as a whole. Being the only one with a positive point of view in the face of negative reactions from others (or vice versa) can cause a respondent to lose their courage.

◆ *Try to listen carefully!*
Listen for more than a confirmation or a validation of your own point of view. Listen to what respondents are actually saying and see things from their perspective. Be willing to listen to misinformation and find in it an insight to the thinking of respondents. If at all possible listen naively: try to forget what you already know and believe; try to leave all your preconceptions outside of the viewing facility! I'm in the habit of saying viewing facilities should have hitching rails outside their doors so people can leave their own hobby horses tethered there.

◆ *Listen to what is and is not being said.*
Try to be alert to the nuances of meaning and the language respondents use to present their perceptions, opinions, beliefs and attitudes. The language used to describe your brand and its competitors can be very valuable in understanding how your brand is really viewed. It is also important to remember that sometimes you can learn as much from what is not said as from what is said.

◆ *Do not expect a consensus within or across groups.*
The degree of divergent thinking may be the trend that needs to be reported. It may be a truism but we are individuals!

◆ *Try to avoid 'judging' respondents.*
It is important to try to avoid judging respondents:

— as 'not worthy' to comment on the content under discussion
— because of the way they look: this could include body type, colour of skin, type of clothing worn, speaking

ability, level of articulateness, style of hair or cosmetics, sexual preferences, regional dialect and so on
— because they do not meet the internal criteria or expectations present in the mind of the observer.

Moderators are encouraged to take a position known as 'unconditional positive regard' (UPR). This guideline if adhered to allows moderators to fully interact with respondents, regardless of our dislike of their looks, speech, attitude, level of participation in the group and so on, as long as they are answering the questions posed and helping reach the intended purpose of the study.

◆ *Watch non-verbal behaviour.*
Look for congruence between what is said and how the respondent looks. Do not 'label' non-verbal behaviour or attach external meanings. For example, a respondent crosses her arms across her chest and leans away from the table as another respondent talks about a sensitive issue. What does her non-verbal behaviour mean? It could mean discomfort with the conversation. It could mean disapproval of the other respondent for having a different point of view and/or for speaking at all about the topic. It could mean an old back injury has flared up and crossing the arms relieves some of the ache. It could mean the yogurt she had before the session is now giving her gas. A wide range of 'possible' explanations exists; therefore, simply note the behaviour and see if verbal comments are made that provide an insight to the 'stance' taken.

◆ *Make your own notes.*
During the discussion process make notes for yourself that will be useful to you in the future. It is easy to forget what was said in the first group half-way through a second one.

◆ *Remember the two-way mirror in a wall is almost impossible to soundproof.*
The following sounds can easily transfer to respondents reminding them of your presence and affecting their replies:

— Clattering cutlery, plates and glasses

— Laughter
— Moving furniture (rocking back and forth in chairs, chair handles bumping into writing counters and so on)
— Rhythmic tapping (for example foot against wall, pencil on counter top and so on).

And finally ... qualitative research is a 'window into the lives of people'

Enjoy the view but do not expect to be entertained. Research is about real people providing their points of view about products, services, ideas, concepts or advertising. Sometimes it is funny; sometimes it is sad; it can be tiresome, exciting and/or enlivening; but it is always about people.

Appendix 3
What are the key dates in a brief history of market research?

A survey of grain production across the United States in 1879 was the subject of what is generally regarded as the first recorded piece of marketing research. It was conducted by one of the first established advertising agencies, N.W. Ayer & Son, so that the agency could develop a better advertising schedule for its clients, the Nichols-Shephard Company, a manufacturer of agricultural machinery.

Year	Activity
1879	First recorded application of market research – N.W. Ayer & Son
1911	First systematic readership survey – Kellogg's
	Bureau of Business Research established at Harvard Graduate School of Business
	Charles Coolidge Parlin is manager of the Commercial Research Division of Curtis Publishing – often called 'the father of market research'
1916	*Chicago Tribune* publishes its survey of households
1924	First independent market research firm set up in UK – H.G. Lyell
1926	American Market Research Council founded
1926–7	Market research first listed as a subject heading in *American Index of Publications*

1928	George Gallup conducts first recorded survey of reader interest in a newspaper
1933	BMRB founded by JWT London
1936	The BBC founds the Listener Research Department (later to become known as Audience Research after the launch of television)
1938	Dr Ernest Dichter founds his Institute for Motivational Research and he helps pioneer and champion the depth interview
1939	AC Nielsen introduces Retail Index (Shop Audit) to UK (Nielsen taken over by Dun & Bradstreet in 1985)
1941	The British Government's Social Survey begins operations
1946	The Market Research Society (MRS) formed with 23 initial members
	Central Office of Information (COI) formed
1948	Attwoods Statistics Ltd operates first consumer household panel in the UK (eventually bought by Audits of Great Britain)
	European Society for Opinion and Marketing Research (ESOMAR) established
1954	MRS Code of Standards adopted
1955	Attwood launch Television Audience Measurement (TAM)
1957	National Opinion Polls (NOP) and Public Attitude Surveys (PAS) both founded
	MRS formally recognised by Board of Trade

1959	First issue of *Commentary* – later renamed *The Journal of the Market Research Society*
	Marplan founded
1960s	Creation of early Simulated Test Market (STM) techniques
1962	Research Bureau Ltd (RBL) formed, later to become Research International (Sold to Ogilvy & Mather in 1986)
	Audits of Great Britain founded, starts TCA panel
1963	Stats MR founded (bought by Nielsen in 1985)
1964	First issue of *The Journal of Marketing Research*
	Association of Market Survey Organisations founded with nine members
1965	Taylor Nelson Associates and Market Behaviour Limited (MBL) both founded (MBL bought by JWT Group in 1979, Taylor Nelson merged with Sofres in 1997)
1966	Retail Audits formed through merger of Test Monitoring Service Ltd and the audit division of the BMRB (becomes part of Nielsen in 1987)
1968	BMRB launches Target Group Index (TGI)
1969	Market and Opinion Research International (MORI), Gordon Simmons Research Group Ltd and Martin-Hamblin all formed
1970s	Rapid growth and development of qualitative research
1970	General Household Survey begins
1971	HMSO publishes first *Social Trends*

1972	RSBG formed
	Stats MR introduces Licensed Trade Audit
1973	Millward Brown Ltd founded (it will become the leading agency in tracking advertising awareness)
1974	Taylor Nelson Family Food Panel formed
1975	Industrial Research Bureau (IRB) formed
1977	AMSO produces its first statistics regarding size of members' turnover. Total market size estimated at £60 million
1978	Hudson Payne Iddiols founded (later to become The HPI Research Group)
1979	CACI Ltd introduces ACORN classification scheme
1980s (onwards)	Increasing centralisation of the industry through buy-outs and mergers, formation of large research organisations led by 'businessmen' (rather than researchers)
1981	The Research Business founded
1982	Association of Qualitative Research Practitioners (AQRP) founded
	◆ RSL takes over Burke ◆ RI takes over Marplan
1984	Data Protection Bill (with implications for both qualitative and quantitative research)
1986	MRS appoints first Director-General

	Unilever sells RI to Ogilvy & Mather (and ultimately WPP when they acquire O&M)
1991	AMSO Research Effectiveness Awards first published
1992	CAPI (Computer Assisted Interviewing) introduced on first omnibus surveys and Readership surveys
1998	New Data Protection Act (which led to comprehensive advice being developed by the MRS for all agencies)
1999	HPI bought by Draft (Part of IPG)
2003	The NFO Group built up by IPG through acquisition is in turn sold to Taylor Nelson Sofres

Bibliography

Allen, Margaret (ed.), *Managing Advertising*, Blackhall Publishing, 1999

Bandler, Richard and John Grinder, *Frogs into Princes*, Real People Press, 1979

Bayley, Stephen, *Labour Camp: The Failure of Style over Substance*, Pan Macmillan, 1998

Birn, Robin, Hague, Paul and Phyllis Vangelder, *A Handbook of Market Research Techniques*, Kogan Page, 1990

Brooks, Libby, 'Melons Feel the squeeze at Tesco', *The Guardian*, 3 May 1999

Buzzell, Robert, 'Is Marketing a Science', *brand strategy*, November 2003

Chisnall, Peter, *Marketing Research: Analysis and Measurement*, McGraw-Hill, 1973

Forrest, Chris and Terry Prue, 'Advertising Research', in Laura Marks (ed.) *Qualitative Research in Context*, Admap Publications, 2000

Gardiner, Sue and Giles Lury, 'The Creative Role of Quantified Research on the Launch of Oxo Gravy Granules', in Derek Martin and C. Ryan (eds) *Research Works 2*, NTC Publications, 1994

Gordon, Wendy, *Good Thinking: A Guide to Qualitative Research*, Admap Publications, 1999

Gordon, Wendy and Roy Langmaid, *Qualitative Research: A Practitioner's and Buyer's Guide*, Goweer Publishing Limited, 1988

Grant, John, *After Image: Mind-altering Marketing*, Profile Business, 2003

Harding, Graham and Paul Walton, *Bluff your Way in Marketing*, Oval Books, 1991

Harris, Paul, 'Sampling and Statistics' in Robin Brin, Paul Hague and Phyllis Vangelder (eds) *A Handbook of Market Research Techniques*, Kogan Page, 1990

Henderson, Naomi, *The Orkla Research Guidelines*, in-house company manual, 2002

Henry, Harry, *Motivational Research*, MCB University Press, 1988

Hine, Thomas, *The Total Package: The Secret History and Hidden Meaning of Boxes, Cans and Other Persuasive Containers*, Back Bay Books; Little, Brown and Company, 1997

Iddiols, David, *Marketing Superglue: How to Make Brand Values Stick*, Admap, May 2000

Johnson, Richard, 'How would you Feel if you Learnt this Man was Studying your Rubbish?' *Sunday Times Magazine*, 2003

Kipling, Rudyard, *The Elephant's Child*, Lectorum Publications, 1990

Kotler, Philip, Armstrong, Gary, Suanders, John and Veronica Wong, *Principles of Marketing*, FT Prentice Hall, 2002

Lewis, Elen, 'Where have all the Ideas Gone?' *brand strategy*, November 2003

Lury, Giles, *Adwatching*, Blackhall Publishing, 2001

Lury, Giles, *Brandwatching* (2nd edn), Blackhall Publishing, 2001

Lury, Giles, 'Time to Do as you Would Be Done By', *Marketing*, 6 February 1997

Market Research Society, Code of Conduct, MRS, 1999

Marks, Laura (ed.), *Qualitative Research in Context*, Admap Publications, 2000

Martin, Derek and Colleen Ryan, *Research Works 2*, NTC Publications, 1994

McDonald, Colin and Stephen King, *Sampling the Universe* (ed. John Goodyear), NTC Publications, 1996

Ogilvy, David, *Ogilvy on Advertising*, Pan, 1983

Perry, Sir M., *The Brand: Vehicle for Value in a Changing Marketplace*, speach to the Advertising Association, 1994

Porter, Michael, *Competitive Advantage*, Free Press, 1985

Rae, John, *New ACORN Groups*, www.caci.co.uk

Ringland, Gill, *Scenario Planning: Managing for the Future*, John Wiley & Sons, 1997

Sampson, Anthony, *Company Man: The Rise and Fall of Corporate Life*, HarperCollins, 1996

Smith, P.R., *Marketing Communications: An Integrated Approach*, Kogan Page, 1993

Social Trends 32, HMSO, 2002

Tuckerman, W.B., *Group Work* (ed. A. Brown), Gower 1986

Wack, Pierre, 'Scenarios: Shooting the Rapids', *Harvard Business Review*, November/December 1985

Wacker, Watts and Jim Taylor, *The 500-Year Delta: What Happens after what Comes Next*, Capstone Publishing, 1997

Walker, David, 'Where have all the Big Ideas Gone?' *brand strategy*

Willke, Joseph, 'The Future of Simulated Test Markets: The Coming Obsolescence of Current Models and the Characteristics of Models of the Future', *ESOMAR*, 2002

Index